This volume
is affectionately
dedicated to
Miss Ruth M. Wardell

Introduction

The personality of Jesus of Nazareth stands as an enigma in Jewish history. Hailed by millions as a Savior and giver of life, his name has been used to condemn the Jews and as an excuse to take Jewish lives.

As a result, except for a few references in the Talmud and in Jewish legends, Jesus was largely ignored by the Jews.

Then came the Enlightenment and the awakening of Jewish nationalism. A flood of books about Jesus issued from Jewish writers somehow trying to make Jesus fit into Jewish history and some attempted to reclaim him for Judaism. In the last two decades, however, this flood has dwindled to a trickle.

But at the turn of the 1970's, the Jewish community was again wrestling with the question of Jesus as Jewish people, young and old, began to accept him and claim him as their Messiah. Rabbis became alarmed and wrote articles of lament against these young people lost to "Judaism and the Jewish people." The Beth Din of Boston decreed that these Jewish believers in Jesus were no longer to be considered Jews, and have forfeited their right to marry Jewish mates or to be buried in a Jewish cemetery. Paradoxically, they added that these same "converts" to Jesus were nevertheless obligated to keep

Jewish law. Odd thing to add if they were no longer Jews.

Soon, every Jewish newspaper across the United States and many of the secular ones began reporting on this new movement of Jews for Jesus. Jesus became an issue in the Jewish community and again it was debated as to exactly where Jesus fits into Jewishness.

This book, rising out of these conflicts in the Jewish community, is an attempt to deal with that very issue.

Acknowledgements in a very special way are made to Miss Vicki Kress for patiently typing the manuscript and making very valuable suggestions in grammar and style.

Unless otherwise stated, all Scripture quotations are from the American Standard Version, 1901 edition.

Contents

1.
What Jewish Leaders Say About Jesus

What do Jews think About Jesus?

There is no uniform Jewish opinion concerning the person of Jesus. The views range from "he never existed" to "a great Jewish prophet." The variety of Jewish views concerning Jesus becomes apparent when one looks through the books on Jesus in a Jewish library. Not uniformity but variety is the term for the understanding of what Jewish writers say about Jesus, as the following quotations will show.

"Since he was regarded as a Jew, there was still within Judaism, at the beginning of the third century, association with the followers of Jesus. One passage in the Talmud seems actually to name the Gospels and quote a specific teaching, but there are opposing opinions about this." [1]

"We sought an answer as to why Judaism did not assent to the Messiahship of Jesus. We found that it was because Jewish tradition did not regard the required messianic conditions as fulfilled with his coming. Judaism, therefore, adhered to the hope that in the days ahead God would bring redemption. But there was no unanimous opinion as to when the Messiah would come and what his exact role would be." [2]

"From Nazareth—a place so unimportant that it is never mentioned in the Old Testament—there arose among the Jewish people a singularly tender and heroic soul. In him

11

religion was the most real thing in life . . . and, although he was only a youth when he launched his public career upon the tempestuous seas of Palestinian affairs, his sympathy for suffering humanity was as ardent as his faith was strong.

"There was something in the character of the man that was overwhelming—a flood of measureless or resistless attractiveness. Unschooled folk from the common walks of life were drawn to him in bonds of personal attachment. Beyond the grave of their buried hopes they clung desperately to his message.

"Jesus himself never wrote a book—not so much as a line—yet it is estimated that more than sixty thousand volumes have been written about him. Eight hundred languages and dialects tell his story. Such is the incomparable grandeur of his influence that for nineteen centuries he has held the undivided interest of men.

"It often happens that he whom one age stones another age enthrones. Less than one hundred years after the man of Nazareth was crucified as a common criminal, people had already magnified him as a supernatural being and were worshipping him as *Very God*. 'The name of Jesus,' once wrote Emensen, 'is not so much written as ploughed into the history of the world.' To me—because I am a Jew—this is an amazing thing, for nothing quite like it has ever happened on so large a scale in the annals of man." [3]

"For nineteen hundred years Jewish history, as wide as it is voluble, has been provokingly silent concerning the most influential Jew the world has ever seen. Of all the amazing things that have happened to Jesus over the centuries, few are as perplexing as this astonishing paradox.

"For Jesus was born a Jew; he lived on the ancestral soil of Palestine, never once setting his foot on alien territory; he taught a small group of disciples, all of whom were as Jewish as he; the language he spoke dripped with Jewish tradition and lore; the little children he loved were

Jewish children; the sinners he associated with were Jewish sinners; he healed Jewish bodies, fed Jewish hunger, poured out wine at a Jewish wedding, and when he died he quoted a passage from the Hebrew book of Psalms. Such a Jew!''[4]

''. . . this scholarship has brought out the fact that Jesus was a Jew, and that his Jewishness was solid to the core—even to the point of sharing contemporary Jewish prejudices. Of course, a great man is always something more than the product of antecedent and surrounding forces. But, be that as it may, no great man can completely transcend his own people. Jesus was born into a definite thought life which was Jewish; he shared the Jewish system of ideas; the only Bible he was familiar with was the Hebrew Old Testament; his apocalyptic ideas were those of his own fellow Palestinians. No Jew was born and reared in the bosom of his people more completely than Jesus. And not until he drew his last breath did he escape being a Jew.''[5]

''Such essays, competently written in the last half-century a great number of times by a great number of able rabbis, normally make two brief points. The first of these is that those Christian views which regard Jesus as more than a man are inconsistent with Judaism and uncongenial to Jews; this view often focuses on the 'Christian Christ.' The second is that those virtues ascribed to Jesus the man, the 'Jewish Jesus,' are characteristic Jewish virtues, expressed in Judaism and integrally a part of it. Such a Jewish Jesus may well have been a good and great man—a prophet, a rabbi or a patriotic leader—but he was not better or greater, say these writings, than other great Jews.''[6]

''When we Jews have understood Christian explanations, and when we have not, we have consistently rejected the Christian claims about Jesus. We have not believed that Jesus was the Messiah; we have not been willing to call him Lord;

we have not believed that the *Logos* became incarnate as
Jesus; we have not believed that Jesus was, or is, the very
Godness of God."[7]

"It seems to me not to violate the documents or that
scholarship which I have imbibed to think of Jesus as some
one who had gifts of leadership and who is something of a
teacher. I believe too that I discern in him a Jewish loyalty at
variance with the views both of Christian and Jewish partisans
who, through opposing motives that cancel each other out,
detach him from Judaism. I believe that Jesus firmly believed
that the end of the world was coming soon. I believe that he
believed himself to be the Messiah, and that those scholars
who deny this are incorrect.

"I own to seeing no originality in the teachings of Jesus.

"I cannot ascribe to the teachings of Jesus a striking
uniqueness in particulars which in honesty I do not discern."[8]

"I discern no possible religious assessment of Jesus, either
by me or by other Jews."[9]

"By his unique personality, Jesus did not fit into any of
these categories. Something of each of these is in him, but he
defies all of them. Men of such extraordinary perception and
passion in the spiritual life of mankind as Jesus was are what
'sports' are in biology."[10]

"Jesus was a Jew and a Jew he remained till his last breath.
His one idea was to implant within his nation the idea of the
coming of the Messiah and, by repentance and good works,
hasten the 'end'."[11]

"The kingdom of heaven, according to Jesus, is in the
present. The kingdom of heaven, according to Judaism, is to
be 'in the latter days.' The former is to come suddenly, 'like a
thief in the night'; the latter will be the fruit of long
development and hard work. True socialism is Jewish and not

Christian. How, then, could Judaism regard Jesus as the Messiah?" 12

" 'Jesus was not a Christian,' but he *became* a Christian. His teaching and his history have been severed from Israel. To this day the Jews have never accepted him, while his disciples and his followers of every generation have scoffed at and persecuted the Jews and Judaism. But even so, we cannot imagine a work of any value touching upon the history of Jews in the time of the Second Temple which does not also include the history of Jesus and an estimate of his teaching. What, therefore, does Jesus stand for in the eyes of the Jews at the present time?

"From the standpoint of general humanity he is, indeed, 'a light to the Gentiles.' His disciples have raised the lighted torch of the Law of Israel (even though that Law has been put forward in a mutilated and incomplete form) among the heathen of the four quarters of the world. No Jew can, therefore, overlook the value of Jesus and his teaching from the point of view of universal history. This is a fact which neither Maimonides nor Yehudah ha-Levi ignored.

"But from the *national Hebrew* standpoint it is more difficult to appraise the value of Jesus. In spite of the fact that he himself was undoubtedly a 'nationalist' Jew by instinct and even an extreme nationalist—as we may see from his retort to the Canaanitish woman, from his depreciatory way of referring to 'the heathen and the publican,' from the terms 'Son of Abraham,' 'Daughter of Abraham' (Which he uses as terms of the highest possible commendation), from his deep love for Jerusalem and from his devoting himself so entirely to the cause of 'the lost sheep of the house of Israel'—in spite of all this, there was in him something out of which arose 'Non-Judaism.' What is Jesus to the *Jewish nation* at the present day?

"To the Jewish nation he can be neither God nor the Son of God, in the sense conveyed by belief in the Trinity. Either conception is to the Jew not only impious and blasphemous, but incomprehensible. Neither can he, to the Jewish nation, be the Messiah: the kingdom of heaven (the 'Days of the Messiah') is not yet come. Neither can they regard him as a Prophet: he lacks the Prophet's political perception and the Prophet's spirit of national consolation in the political-national sense.

"Neither can they regard him as a lawgiver or the founder of a new religion: he did not even desire to be such. Neither is he a *'Tanna,'* or Pharisaic rabbi: he nearly always ranged himself in opposition to the Pharisees and did not apprehend the positive side in their work, the endeavour to take within their scope the entire national life and to strengthen the national existence.

"But Jesus is, for the Jewish nation, *a great teacher of morality and an artist in parable.* He is *the* moralist for whom, in the religious life, morality counts as—everything. Indeed, as a consequence of this extremist standpoint his ethical code has become simply an ideal for the isolated few, a 'Zukunfts-Musik,' an ideal for 'the days of the Messiah,' when an 'end' shall have been made of this 'old world,' this present social order. It is no ethical code for the nations and the social order of to-day, when men are still trying to find the way to that future of the Messiah and the Prophets, and to the 'kingdom of the Almighty' spoken of by the *Talmud,* an ideal which is of 'this world' and which, gradually and in the course of generations, is to take shape in this world.

"But in his ethical code there is a sublimity, distinctiveness and originality in form unparalleled in any other Hebrew ethical code; neither is there any parallel to the remarkable art of his parables. The shrewdness and sharpness of his proverbs and his forceful epigrams serve, in an exceptional degree, to make ethical ideas a popular possession. If ever the day should come and this ethical code be stripped of its wrappings of miracles and mysticism, the Book of the Ethics of Jesus will be one of the choicest treasures in the literature of Israel for all time." [13]

"Jesus, the Jesus of the Gospels, only Son and Incarnation of God for the Christians, in his human lifetime was a Jew, a humble Jewish artisan. This is a fact of which no Christian has a right to be unaware.

"Everything we know about Jesus shows that he was Jewish. Not only Jewish by belief, by religion. Jewish by birth." [14]

"Insofar as we can know of them through the Gospels, Jesus' family was Jewish: Mary, his mother, was Jewish, and so were all their friends and relatives. To be at once an anti-Semite and a Christian is to try to marry reverence with abuse." [15]

"Nothing would be more futile than to try to separate from Judaism the Gospel that Jesus preached in the synagogues and in the Temple. The truth is that the Gospel and its entire tradition are deeply rooted in Jewish tradition and in the attempts at renovation and purification which had been manifested for almost two centuries in Palestine." [16]

"The story of Jesus is, then, a simple one, understandable in terms of modern political experience, and probably little different from the numerous other Jewish Zealots who led groups of rebels to martyrdom and crucifixion. In the real life of Jesus we can discern nothing supernatural, no theology, no dogma, only zeal for his people and his God." [17]

"But interreligious understanding based on mutual respect is not a one-way street. We Jews have long clamored for this indispensable change in official Catholic dissemination of facts and interpretation. But what about our Jewish attitudes toward Christendom, toward Jesus especially? Are we to remain adamant—orthodox—in our refusal to examine our own statements, our own facts, our own interpretations of the significance of the life of Jesus, the Jew? Have we examined our own books, official and otherwise, to reappraise our oft-times jaundiced view of him in whose name Christianity was established? How long can we persist in ignoring his lofty and yet so simply stated prophetic and rabbinic teachings, merely on the grounds that he repeated much that was voiced by his prophetic predecessors and rabbinic contemporaries? Was Micah more spiritually and morally original than Amos and Hosea? Do none of the rabbis we revere and whose utterances we have our children master repeat each other?

"How long shall we continue pompously to aver that the chief contribution of Jesus was simply a rehash of all that had been said before by his Jewish ancestors? How long before we can admit that his influence was a beneficial one—not only to the pagans but to the Jews of his time as well, and that only those who later took his name in vain profaned his teaching?

"We have been—not without much justice—constantly on the *qui vive* to fend off what we have, often rightly, regarded as insulting and demeaning slurs upon us and upon our faith. But I would hope that we, too, have grown up sufficiently in our religious security and as the world's most adult religion in terms of seniority, that we can now afford to render unto Jesus that which is Jesus's without blanching or self-flagellation." [18]

"To Jews, that Jesus appears as an extraordinarily beautiful and noble spirit, aglow with life and pity for men, especially for the unfortunate and lost, deep in piety, of keen insight into human nature, endowed with a brilliant gift of parable and epigram, an ardent Jew moreover, a firm believer in the faith of his people; all in all, a dedicated teacher of the principles, religious and ethical, of Judaism. But is he not something more than a teacher? Should he not be taken for a moral prophet also, one who promulgated new, higher, hitherto unknown principles of conduct?

"Not if the record is examined objectively."[19]

"But will not Jews accept him, if not as a prophet, then at least as a perfect man, an ideal for all to imitate?

"That too is not tenable. The sober truth is that Jesus, spiritual hero that he is, is not perfect."[20]

"Very well then, says the Christian, let it be conceded that Jesus is neither God, nor uniquely His son, nor the Messiah, nor a moral prophet, nor even an impeccable human being.

"Certainly he was, despite his defects, a great man, a gifted and exalted teacher. Will not the Jews accept him as such?

"To which the answer of Jews runs: 'Have Jews, except under the extremist provocation, ever quarreled with such a presentation of him?' "[21]

"Enough evidence has been presented that Jesus, as represented by the Gospels, had placed himself outside the synagogue and the Jewish people."[22]

If these quotations show anything, it is to reveal that there is no such thing as *the* Jewish view of Jesus. Not uniformity but variety is the dominant theme. To some he was a great Jewish moralist, teacher, and prophet who was responsible for the spread of Jewish ideas among the Gentiles. To others he was little more than a parrot repeating ideas of other rabbis, showing no originality of his own. To some he was a Jewish patriot who was born a Jew, lived a zealous Jewish life, and died a Jew. To others, though he was born a Jew, he became a non-Jew and placed himself outside the fold of Judaism.

To virtually all, whoever he was, rightly or wrongly, they concluded that he was not the Messiah. He did not fulfill the messianic requirements and therefore could not be the Messiah.

But what are these messianic requirements by which Jesus is adjudged not to be the Messiah?

Whatever they are, there is only one source to discover them. This source is the Hebrew Scriptures, commonly referred to as the Old Testament. If there is an objective standard for messianic expectations, this is it. There is no other option or source to turn to. Therefore, to these we now turn to see what the Messiah of the Old Testament was really to be like.

NOTES

1. Rabbi Morris Goldstein, *Jesus in the Jewish Tradition* (New York: Macmillan Company, 1950), p. 232.

2. *Ibid.,* p. 233.

3. Ernest R. Trattner, *As A Jew Sees Jesus* (New York: Charles Scribner's Sons, 1931), pp. ix-x.

4. *Ibid.,* p. 1.

5. *Ibid.,* pp. 19-20.

6. Samuel Sandmel, *We Jews and Jesus* (New York: Oxford University Press, 1965), p. vii.

7. *Ibid.,* p. 44.

8. *Ibid.,* p. 109.

9. *Ibid.,* p. 110.

10. Beryl D. Cohon, *Men at the Crossroads* (New York: Thomas Yoseloff, 1970), p. 114.

11. Joseph Klausner, *Jesus of Nazareth* (New York: Macmillan Company, 1925), p. 368.

12. *Ibid.,* p. 406.

13. *Ibid.,* pp. 413-14.

14. Jules Isaac, *Jesus and Israel* (New York: Holt, Rinehart, and Winston, 1971), p. 11.

15. *Ibid.,* p. 15.

16. *Ibid.,* p. 74.

17. Simon S. Levin, *Jesus Alias Christ* (New York: Philosophical Library, 1969), p. 71.

18. Maurice Eisendrath, *Jewry and Jesus of Nazareth* (England: the Parkes Library, 1964), p. 6.

19. Rabbi Milton Steinberg, "Basic Judaism," *Jewish Information,* Vol. 3, No. 4, Spring, 1963, p. 37.

20. *Ibid.,* p. 39.

21. *Ibid.,* p. 40.

22. Trude Weiss-Rosmarin, "Why Jews Don't Accept Jesus," *The Jewish Digest,* June, 1973, p. 27.

2.
The Messiah of the Old Testament
Part 1: The Conflict of Isaiah 53

The Paradox

Anyone who sets himself to the task of seeking to know what the Old Testament has to say about the coming of the Messiah soon finds himself involved with a seeming paradox. At times one even seems to be faced with an outright contradiction. For the Jewish prophets gave a two-fold picture of the Messiah who was to come.

On the one hand, the inquirer will find numerous predictions regarding the Messiah which portray him as one who is going to suffer humiliation, physical harm, and finally death in a violent manner. This death was stated by the Jewish prophets to be a substitutionary death for the sins of the Jewish people. On the other hand, he will find that the Jewish prophets also spoke of the Messiah coming as a conquering king who will destroy the enemies of Israel and set up the messianic kingdom of peace and prosperity.

This is the two-fold picture the Jewish prophets gave of the Messiah. For centuries past, during the formulation of the *Talmud,* our rabbis made serious studies of messianic prophecies. They came up with this conclusion: The prophets spoke of *two different Messiahs.*

The Messiah who was to come, suffer and die was termed Messiah, the Son of Joseph *(Mashiach ben Yo-*

seph). The second Messiah who would then come following the first was termed Messiah, the Son of David
(Mashiach ben David). This one would raise the first
Messiah back to life, and establish the Messianic kingdom of peace on earth. That the Old Testament presents
these two lines of Messianic prophecy was something
that all the early rabbis recognized. The Old Testament
never clearly states that there will be two Messiahs. In
fact, many of the paradoxical descriptions are found
side by side in the same passages, in which it seems
that only one person is meant. But for the early rabbis
the two-Messiahs theory seemed to be the best answer.

For centuries Orthodox Judaism held the concept of
two Messiahs. Since the Talmudic period, however, in
the history of the Jewish people the Son of David alone
was played up in the imaginations of Jewish hearts and
minds. The other messianic figure, Messiah, the Son
of Joseph, the suffering one, was ignored, He was there
in Jewish theology when needed to explain the suffering
Messiah passages contained in the Old Testament. His
existence provided an escape clause when thorny questions were raised. Otherwise this Messianic figure was
largely ignored. Today, few Jews have heard of him
or know of his existence in Jewish theology of days gone
by. The one that Jews today know of is the one who
is to conquer: Messiah, the Son of David.

The Source of the Paradox

One of the major sources from which the rabbis developed their concept of the suffering Messiah, the Son
of Joseph, was Isaiah 53. The present-day bone of contention regarding what the Old Testament says about

the Messiah centers on this chapter. The passage speaks of a servant, the Servant of Jehovah. This servant undergoes a great deal of suffering ending in death. The chapter goes on to state that this suffering is a vicarious suffering, that the death is a substitutionary death for sin. He is suffering and dying for the sins of others. The passage goes on to indicate that this servant is resurrected. The bone of contention is not so much over *what* the passage says but of *whom* does it speak.

The question today concerns of whom Isaiah was speaking. Did he prophecy concerning the Messiah here? Rabbis say that this is the *Christian* interpretation of this passage and not the *Jewish* one. The *Jewish* interpretation, they would say, is that Isaiah is speaking about the people of Israel, the Jewish people suffering in the Gentile world. This is *the* Jewish interpretation, the rabbis would say—and it does not speak of the Messiah at all.

But to make the passage speak of the collective body of Israel seems almost to force an interpretation. Taken by itself, the passage seems to have only one individual in mind.

Rabbinical Interpretations of Isaiah 53

But is this conflict merely between the Jewish interpretation and the Christian one? The history of Judaism shows otherwise. The interpretation that Isaiah 53 is referring to the Jewish people is really a recent one. The original interpretation of Isaiah 53 by Jewish rabbis has been that it is speaking of an individual—the Messiah himself. In fact, the concept of Messiah, the Son of Joseph, comes from this passage. But for a clearer

idea of what the old Jewish view of Isaiah 53 was, it
would be good to turn to history.

Among the earliest *Targums* are those of Jonathan ben
Uzziel dating from the first century A.D. His *Targums* on
this passage of Isaiah begin with these words: "Behold
my servant Messiah shall prosper. . . ." The *Targums* of
Jonathan ben Uzziel were heavily quoted by the early
rabbis and he was certainly considered an authority on
the Jewish view of Scripture. He definitely considered the
Isaiah passage to speak of Messiah. Jonathan ben Uzziel
could hardly be accused of adopting the "Christian
interpretation."

That Jonathan ben Uzziel was not alone in this interpretation becomes clear from a quotation from Rabbi
Don Yitzchak Abarbanel from about 1500. While he
himself did not accept the view that the Isaiah passage
referred to the Messiah, he makes a dramatic admission:

> The first question is to ascertain to whom (this scripture)
> refers: for the learned among the Nazarenes expound it of the
> man who was crucified in Jerusalem at the end of the second
> temple and who according to them was the Son of God and
> took flesh in the virgin's womb as it is stated in their writings.
> Jonathan ben Uzziel interpreted it in the Targum of the future
> Messiah; *but this is also the opinion of our learned men in the
> majority of the midrashim* (italics added).

In spite of Abarbanel's personal view regarding this
passage, he freely admits that the majority of the rabbis
of the *Midrashim* took the passage to speak of the
Messiah. He thus points out that Jonathan ben Uzziel
was not alone in his opinion but rather this was *the*

Jewish view of the period of the *Targumim* and the *Midrashim.*

The *Zohar,* thought to have been written either by Simon ben Yochai in the second century or by a Spanish rabbi in the thirteenth century, makes certain statements which have obvious references to the Isaiah passage:

> There is in the garden of Eden a palace called the Palace of the sons of sickness; this palace the Messiah then enters, and summons every sickness, every pain, and every chastisement of Israel; they all come and rest upon him. And were it not that he had thus lighted them off Israel and taken them upon himself, there had been no man able to bear Israel's chastisement for transgression of the law: and this is that which is written, "Surely our sickness he had carried."

The *Zohar* in this quotation quotes from Isaiah 53:4 and referred the passage to the Messiah himself. The passage further makes Israel distinct from the one referred to in the Isaiah passage. Furthermore, the *Zohar* recognizes the vicariousness and substitutional element in the passage—the Messiah is taking upon himself the suffering due to Israel for their sins.

More evidence from within the same period is provided by the *Talmud:* "The Messiah—what is his name? . . . those of the house of Rabbi Yuda the Saint say, The sick one, as it is said, "Surely he had borne our sicknesses" (98$_b$).

Like the *Zohar,* the *Babylonian Talmud* also took the Isaiah passage to refer to the Messiah. Verse 4 is specifically applied to the person of the Messiah himself.

In *Midrash Thanhumi* we find:

> Rabbi Nahman says, the word "man" in the passage . . .

refers to the Messiah, the son of David, as it is written, "Behold the *man* whose name is Zemah"; there Jonathan interprets, Behold the man Messiah; as it is said, "a man of pains and known to sickness."

The *Targums Yalkut* II:338:7 refers Isaiah 52:13 to the Messiah and says of this passage: "He shall be exalted and extolled—He shall be higher than Abraham, higher than Moses, higher than the ministering angels."

The *Midrash Cohen,* when dealing with Isaiah 53:5, puts the following words in the mouth of Elijah the prophet. Elijah says to Messiah: "Bear the suffering and punishment of thy Lord, with which he chastises thee for the sins of Israel, as it is written, 'He is pressed for our rebellion—crushed for our iniquities' until the end come."

Another *Midrash* on this same passage states: "All the sufferings are divided into three parts. One part goes to David and the Patriarchs, another to the generation of the rebellion (rebellious Israel) and the third to King Messiah."

Another volume that takes the Isaiah passage to refer to the Messiah is the *Mahsor* or the Prayer Book for the Day of Atonement. One of the many prayers found in this volume is called the Musaf Prayer. It was written by Rabbi Eliezer Kalir around the seventh century A.D. Part of the prayer reads as follows:

Messiah our Righteousness is departed from us: horror hath seized us, and we have none to justify us. He hath borne the yoke of our iniquities, and our transgression, and was wounded because of our transgression. He beareth our sins on his shoulder, that he may find pardon for our iniquities. We shall be healed by his wound, at the time that the Eternal will create him (the Messiah) as a new creature. O bring him up from the circle of the earth, Raise him up from the land of Seir, to assemble us on Mount Lebanon, a second time by the power of Yinon.

The more this Yom Kippur prayer is studied, the more interesting it becomes. The prayer voices fear that the Messiah has departed from the people, which assumes that Messiah had already come to them and has left them. Furthermore, the Messiah who has departed has suffered vicariously for the people, the sins of the people having been placed on this Messiah. Now after suffering, the Messiah has departed from them; this is the cause of their consternation. Now the people pray for the Messiah to come back a second time. Much of this prayer is a direct quotation from the Isaiah passage. This shows therefore that even as late as the seventh century, the Jewish view was still that this passage had reference to the Messiah.

That this view was still the dominant one among Jewry in the tenth century is seen from the commentary of Yepheth ben 'All:

As for myself, I am inclined with Benjamin of Nehavend, to regard it as alluding to the Messiah . . . He (the prophet) thus gives us to understand two things: In the first instance, that the Messiah will only reach his highest degree of honor after long and severe trials; and secondly, that these trials will be sent upon him as a kind of sign, so that, if he finds himself under the yoke of misfortunes while remaining pious in his actions, he may know that he is the designated one. . . . The expression "my servant" is applied to the Messiah as it is applied to his ancestor in the verse, "I have sworn to David my servant."

This rabbi, too, recognized the passage to be in reference to the Messiah. He makes the point in accordance with the passage that the Messiah will reach his high state of glory by means of suffering.

Jews in the eleventh century also considered the passage to speak of the Messiah. In the *Bereshith Rabbah* of Rabbi Moshe Hadarshan we find these words:

> The Holy One gave Messiah the opportunity to save souls but to be severely chastised: and forthwith the Messiah accepted the chastisements of love, as it is written, "He was oppressed, and he was afflicted." And when Israel is sinful, the Messiah seeks mercy upon them, as it is written, "By his stripes we were healed," and, "He carried the sins of many and made intercession for the transgressors."

By quoting from Isaiah 53, verses 7, 5, and 12 respectively, the author of *Bereshith Rabbah* draws certain conclusions. One is that the Messiah will save many, but that this salvation of the many is accomplished by means of his suffering. Secondly, the Messiah's sufferings are viewed to be vicarious in nature, for he is seen as suffering for the sins of Israel.

Another rabbi from the eleventh century, Rabbi Tobiyyah ben Eliezer, in his *Legah Tova* has this to say about Isaiah 52:13: "And let his kingdom be exalted," in the days of the Messiah, of whom it is said, "Behold my servant shall prosper; he will be high and *exalted,* and lofty exceedingly."

Among the most famous rabbis of this period was Moses ben Maimon, better known as Maimonides or the Rambam. In his writings he, too, makes the Isaiah passage refer to the Messiah:

Regarding the mission by which Messiah will present himself, . . . he will not commend himself to our veneration by reason of his notable extraction; but the marvelous deeds he shall perform will show him to be the anticipated Messiah . . . Isaiah states, "He grew like a tender plant, and as a root out of dry land," signifying, that his exact descent will not be known, till his successful career will direct people's attention to it. . . . But a noteworthy circumstance will be that crowned heads will stand amazed. . . . So they will remain in utter silence, as Isaiah predicts, "At him will kings shut their mouths, for what had not been told unto them shall they see, and what they never heard shall they understand."

The Rambam quotes from Isaiah 53:2 and 52:15 respectively and refers these passages to the Messiah's person. This is his view regarding the entire passage.

Also from the eleventh century, an ancient Jewish writing states concerning the Messiah:

Messiah, the son of Ephraim, will die there, and Israel will mourn for him. And afterwards the Holy One will reveal to them Messiah, the son of David, whom Israel will decide to stone, saying, Thou spakest falsely: already is the Messiah slain. . . . and so they will despise him, as it is written, "Despised and rejected of men."

The writer presents the Two Messiahs view which was the common Jewish view of his day. One Messiah, the Son of Ephraim or Joseph, will die. After his death will come the Messiah, the Son of David whom, the rabbi says, Israel will reject. He quotes from Isaiah 53:3 to prove his point.

During this time, we have for the first time in the history of Jewish theology the idea that this passage

was not in reference to the Messiah but in reference
to the people of Israel. It was first propounded by Rabbi
Shlomoh Yizchaki, better known as Rashi. But since
he went contrary to the traditional Jewish view concerning this passage, there was an immediate reaction by
other Jewish authorities.

One rabbi who reacted against the new view propounded by Rashi was Rabbi Moshe Kohen Ibn Crispin
of Cordova and Toledo in Spain at about 1350:

> I am pleased to interpret it in accordance of our Rabbis,
> of the King Messiah, and will be careful, so far as I am able,
> to adhere to the literal sense: thus, possibly, I shall be free
> from the fancied and far fetched interpretations of which
> others have been guilty.
>
> This prophecy was delivered by Isaiah at the divine com-
> mand for the purpose of making known to us something about
> the nature of the future Messiah, who is to come and deliver
> Israel, and his life for the day when he arrives at discretion
> until his advent as a redeemer, in order that if any one should
> arise claiming to be himself the Messiah, we may reflect, and
> look to see whether we can observe in him any resemblance
> to the traits described here: if there is any such resemblance,
> then we may believe that he is the Messiah our righteousness;
> but if not, we cannot do so.

The "fancied and far fetched" interpretation that
Rabbi Crispin has reference to is the interpretation of
Rashi that this does not refer to the Messiah but to
the people of Israel. This rabbi reacts against this interpretation and insists that this Isaiah passage refers
to Messiah, that it was written for the purpose of helping
identify the Messiah so that he can be recognized when
he comes.

In the sixteenth century we have the words of Rabbi Saadyeh Ibn Danan of Grenada, c. 1500:

> One of these, Rabbi Joseph ben Kaspi, was led so far as to say that those who expounded it of the Messiah, who is shortly to be revealed, gave occasion to the heretics to interpret it of Jesus. May God, however, forgive him for not having spoken the truth! Our Rabbis, the doctors of the Talmud, delivered their opinions by the power of prophecy, possess a tradition concerning the principles of interpretation. . . . alludes solely to the King Messiah.

This Rabbi also reacts against the interpretation that the Isaiah passage refers to the people of Israel. He demands that Jewish interpreters return to the Talmudic interpretation that this refers to the Messiah. He also helps to shed some light as to the reason why many were switching over to the new view. It was during this period that many debates broke out between rabbis and Christians, and the latter used Isaiah 53 to show that Jesus was the Messiah. Because of the force of their arguments, as a defense rabbis began to refer the passage to Israel.

Also from the second half of the sixteenth century are the writings of Rabbi Moshe Le Sheich (Al Shech), who was a disciple of Joseph Caro, author of the *Shulchan Aruch*. He, too, demanded that all Jewish interpreters return to the more traditional interpretation when he wrote: "Our Rabbis of blessed memory with one voice accept and affirm the opinion that the prophet is speaking of the King Messiah. And we ourselves shall also adhere to the same view."

The writings of Rabbi Eliyyah de Vidas are from

about the same time. He wrote the following c. 1575 concerning Isaiah 53:5:

> But he was wounded for our transgressions, bruised for our iniquities, the meaning of which is that since the Messiah bears our iniquities which produce the effect of his being bruised, it follows that whoso will not admit that the Messiah thus suffers for our iniquities, must endure and suffer them himself.

This rabbi, too, refers the passage to the Messiah and states that the Messiah will suffer vicariously, for he suffers for the sins of the people. The Rabbi goes on to say that those who refuse to believe and accept the vicarious suffering for sin which the Messiah bore are doomed, according to the passage, to suffer for their own sins.

Even in the seventeenth century there was still reaction against Rashi's interpretation of the Isaiah passage, as the writing of Rabbi Naphtali ben Asher Altschuler (c. 1650) shows: "I will proceed to explain these verses of our own Messiah, who, God willing, will come speedily in our days. I am surprised that Rashi and Rabbi David Kimchi have not, with the Targums, applied it to the Messiah likewise."

By the nineteenth century, the new view propounded by Rashi and followed by Rabbi David Kimchi had pretty well won over the older view of the rabbis. But the victory was not total, for there was still a reaction against it. Herz Homburg in his *Korem*, written in 1818, wrote: "The fact is, that it refers to the King Messiah, who will come in the latter days, when it will be the Lord's good pleasure to redeem Israel from among the different nations of the earth."

So to interpret Isaiah 53 as speaking of Messiah is not non-Jewish. In fact, if we are to speak of the *traditional* Jewish interpretation, it would be that the passage speaks of the Messiah. The first one to expound the view that this referred to Israel rather than the Messiah was Shlomo Yizchaki, better known as Rashi (c. 1040-1105). He was followed by David Kimchi (1160-1235). But this was to go contrary to all rabbinical teaching of that day and of the preceding one thousand years. Today, Rashi's view has become dominant in Jewish and rabbinical theology. But that is not *the* Jewish view. Nor is it the *traditional* Jewish view. Those closer to the time of the original writings, and who had less contact with the Christian apologists, interpreted it as speaking of the Messiah.

The Text of Isaiah 52:13 to 53:12

The text itself should be able to help us determine whether the Suffering Servant is the individual Messiah or the nation of Israel. Before dealing with some specific details given in the text, it might prove helpful to quote the entire Isaiah passage and then make a summary of it.

Behold, my servant shall deal wisely, he shall be exalted and lifted up, and shall be very high. Like as many were astonished at thee, (his visage was so marred more than any man, and his form more than the sons of men,) so shall he sprinkle many nations; kings shall shut their mouths at him: for that which had not been told them shall they see; and that which they had not heard shall they understand.

Who hath believed our message? and to whom hath the

arm of Jehovah been revealed? For he grew up before him as a tender plant, and as a root out of a dry ground: he hath no form nor comeliness; and when we see him, there is no beauty that we should desire him. He was despised, and rejected of men; a man of sorrows, and acquainted with grief: and as one from whom men hide their face he was despised; and we esteemed him not.

Surely he hath borne our griefs, and carried our sorrows; yet we did esteem him stricken, smitten of God, and afflicted. But he was wounded for our transgressions, he was bruised for our iniquities; the chastisement of our peace was upon him; and with his stripes we are healed. All we like sheep have gone astray; we have turned every one to his own way; and Jehovah hath laid on him the iniquity of us all.

He was oppressed, yet when he was afflicted he opened not his mouth; as a lamb that is led to the slaughter, and as a sheep that before its shearers is dumb, so he opened not his mouth. By oppression and judgment he was taken away; and as for his generation, who among them considered that he was cut off out of the land of the living for the transgression of my people to whom the stroke was due? And they made his grave with the wicked, and with a rich man in his death; although he had done no violence, neither was any deceit in his mouth.

Yet it pleased Jehovah to bruise him; he hath put him to grief: when thou shalt make his soul an offering for sin, he shall see his seed, he shall prolong his days, and the pleasure of Jehovah shall prosper in his hand. He shall see of the travail of his soul, and shall be satisfied: by the knowledge of himself shall my righteous servant justify many; and he shall bear their iniquities. Therefore will I divide him a portion with the great, and he shall divide the spoil with the strong; because he poured out his soul unto death, and was numbered with the transgressors: yet he bare the sin of many, and made intercession for the transgressors.

Summary of the Contents of the Passage

In Isaiah 52:13-15 God is doing the speaking. He is calling the attention of all to the Suffering Servant. God declares that his Servant will act wisely and his actions will gain him a position of glory. God further states that his Servant will suffer, but this suffering will eventually gain the silent attention of world rulers when they begin to understand the purpose of his suffering. The Servant will be terribly disfigured but will in the end save many.

After God has thus drawn the attention of the people to his Servant, the people now respond in 53:1-9. In verses 1-3 they confess their nonrecognition of the Servant in his person and calling. In verse 1 they claim to be surprised at what they had just learned from the three preceeding verses. In verse 2, they note that at the time that the Servant was with them, there did not seem to be anything special about him. His childhood and growth were no different than those of others. He was not particularly charismatic in his personality that it would attract men to him. His outward features were hardly unique. On the contrary, verse 3 points out that the opposite was true. Instead of drawing the people to him, he was despised and rejected by men in general. He was a man of sorrows, acquainted with personal grief. His rejection was not merely passive; it was active, and the people did their best to avoid him.

In verses 4-6, the people confess that at the time of his suffering, they considered his suffering to be the punishment of God for his own sins. Now, however, they acknowledge that the Servant's suffering was vi-

carious: He suffered for the sins of the people and not
for his own sins. The people confess that it was they
who went astray; they each one had gone their own
selfish ways, and the punishment of their sins was laid
upon the Servant of Jehovah. This passage, then, is a
confession of a change of attitude on the part of the
people towards the Servant as they recognized the true
nature of his sufferings. The severe judgment which the
Servant had suffered led the people to form an opinion
of him, since his suffering seemed to mark him out as
a special victim of Jehovah's anger. But now confession
is made concerning the reversal of this opinion, which
marks the beginning of repentance.

In verse 4 those who formerly misunderstood and
despised the Servant on account of his miserable condi-
tion now are better instructed. They now recognize that
the Servant of Jehovah was vicariously suffering for
them and took upon himself what was actually due to
them. They confess that his sufferings were of an altogether different nature from what they had supposed.
They are now bearing witness against themselves, la-
menting their former blindness to the mediatorial and
vicarious character of the deep agonies of body and
soul that were involved in the suffering. The error being
confessed is that they had considered his sufferings as
a punishment for sins he himself had committed.

In verse 5 the people confess that the vicarious suffering of the Servant of Jehovah resulted in reconciliation
and spiritual healing. This verse penetrates more deeply
into the meaning of the Servant's sufferings, seeing the
connection between his passion and their sins. The connection is two-fold: *Chastisement for our sins*—suffering

was the penalty for the people's transgression; *Means of Reconciliation*—it was the remedy by which the people are restored to spiritual health. It was for the sins of the people that he was suffering and not for his own sins.

In verse 6 the people confess that the necessity of the sufferings spoken of in the preceding verses was that the people were so wholly estranged from God that substitution was required for reconciliation. They had strayed and selfishly sought their own way; yet Jehovah laid their sins on the Servant. Thus the people confess with penitence that they have long mistaken him whom God has sent to them for their good, even when they had gone astray to their own ruin.

In verses 7-9 the prophet appears to be doing the speaking as he describes and details the sufferings of the Servant that lead to his death.

In verse 7, the Servant is pictured as humbly submitting himself to unjust treatment. He does not speak a word in his own defense. He suffers quietly, never crying out against the injustice done to him.

In verse 8, we find the death of the Servant of Jehovah. Here we are told that after a judicial trial and judgment, he was taken away for execution. The Servant of Jehovah was being executed for the sins of the prophet's own people, who were the ones who deserved the judgment of judicial execution. But no one seemed to realize the holy purpose of God in this event. Verse 8 is a key verse to the entire passage, in that we learn that this was a sentence of death pronounced in a court of law and then executed. This verse clearly states that he did not deserve the death. Those for whom he was dying never realized the true reason for his death. But, as verses 4-6 have related, they assumed he was dying for his own sins.

In verse 9, the burial of the Servant is described. After his death, those who executed him assigned a criminal's grave for him along with other criminals. A criminal is what they considered him to be, and that is the way he was executed. Yet he would be buried in a rich man's tomb! This is true poetic justice, since in actuality the Servant had done nothing wrong, nor was there anything wrong in his character.

In verses 10-12 we have the results of the sufferings and death of the Servant of Jehovah. These results in the end are very benefical.

In verse 10 it is recorded how God was pleased to allow the Servant to suffer and die. This was the means by which God was going to make the atonement for the people. The death of the Servant was an offering for the sins of the people. The ones who had gone astray and sinned would now be forgiven on the basis of the death of the Servant, for by his substitutionary death he provided the atonement for the people. God punished the Servant in place of the people and thus the sins of the people were atoned for. This verse further states that the Servant will see his posterity and his days will be prolonged. How can that be if the Servant is killed? The only way that this would be possible is by means of resurrection. So the pleasure of the Lord, the verse concludes, will continue to prosper in his hand, for he will live again because of his resurrection.

Verse 11 declares that God will be satisfied with the work of the Servant. The Servant of Jehovah dies a substitutionary death for the sins of the people. The question now is: Will God accept this substitution? And the answer is yes. For God will see the sufferings and death of the Servant and his justice will be satisfied. Therefore God can make the next statement, that because of his vicarious suffering and death, the righteous Servant will justify many. To justify means to declare righteous. So the Servant who suffered and died and is now resurrected will be able to make many righteous. The people who were sinners and could do nothing because of separation from God will be able to be made righteous by the Servant. This verse concludes by telling us how this is possible—the servant bears their sins. Their sins are put on the Servant's account, and the account is considered paid in full by the Servant's blood. So God declares that his righteous Servant will cause many to be justified in the knowledge of himself, for he will bear their sins.

Verse 12 records that the Servant will be tremendously and greatly blessed by God in the end above all others. The reasons for this are given in the verse. First of all, he willingly and voluntarily suffered and died. Secondly, he was humble enough to allow others to consider him a sinner and to consider him as suffering and dying for his own sins. However, thirdly, he actually "Bare the sin of many." For the many who are justified and made righteous are so only because he has put their sins on his account. Fourthly, and finally, the Servant makes intercession and pleads to God on behalf of the sinners.

This, essentially, is the summary of what the content of the passage is. If the Servant is Israel, the people are the Gentiles. If the Servant is the Messiah, then the people are Israel, the Jewish people. Until Rashi, all Jewish theology taught that this referred to the Messiah. Since Rashi, most of rabbinical theology has taught that it refers to Israel. If the passage is taken literally and read simply, it speaks of a single individual.

Clues to Interpretation

The text itself provides a number of clues as to which is really meant. In itself, it makes plain whether an individual Messiah is being referred to or the collective body of Israel.

An important clue as to whom this passage refers is the consistent usage of pronouns. A distinction is maintained between WE, US, and OUR as over against HE, HIM, and HIS. The use of WE, US, and OUR in the passage must refer to Isaiah the Prophet and the people to whom Isaiah is speaking. The use of HE, HIM, and HIS must refer to the Suffering Servant. Now Isaiah was a Jew, as were also the people to whom he was speaking. It will be good to requote a portion of this passage to bring out the emphasis of the various pronouns in order to get a clearer understanding of the point being made. The following quotation is Isaiah 53:4-9:

Surely HE hath borne OUR griefs, and carried OUR sorrows; yet WE did esteem HIM stricken, smitten of God, and afflicted. But HE was wounded for OUR transgressions, HE was bruised for OUR iniquities; the chastisement of OUR peace was upon HIM; and with HIS stripes WE are healed. All WE like sheep have gone astray; WE have turned every one to his own way; and Jehovah hath laid on HIM the iniquity of US all.

HE was oppressed, yet when HE was afflicted HE opened not HIS mouth; as a lamb that is led to the slaughter, and as a sheep that before its shearers is dumb, so HE opened not HIS mouth. By oppression and judgment HE was taken away; and as for HIS generation, who among THEM considered that HE was cut off out of the land of the living for the transgression of MY people to whom the stroke was due? And THEY made HIS grave with the wicked, and with a rich man in HIS death; although HE had done no violence, neither was any deceit in HIS mouth.

Obviously the WE, US, and OUR are the Jews. Isaiah and the people are the Jews. Isaiah is speaking to the nation of Israel, the Jewish people as a whole. He is including himself with the collective body of Israel. Isaiah represents the Suffering Servant as being in a different category: HE, HIM, and HIS. HE is the one who is suffering for US. HE is the one God is laying OUR sins upon. HE is the one who is going to die for OUR sins so that WE can have salvation through HIM. The constant and consistant use of pronouns and the identification of the pronouns exclude the Suffering Servant from being Israel. Rather, the Suffering Servant is the Messiah himself.

The second clue is the closing sentence of verse 8, which also serves to exclude Israel from being the Suffering Servant. It reads: ". . . he was cut off out of the land of the living for the transgression of my people to whom the stroke was due."

As Isaiah the prophet views the death of the Suffering Servant, he discloses that his death is for the sins of "my people." Who are Isaiah's people? No one questions that Isaiah was a Jew. Thus, Isaiah's people must be the Jews; they must be the people of Israel as well. And if "my people" are Israel, they cannot be the Suffering Servant. Hence, the Suffering Servant must refer to the individual Messiah.

A third clue lies in the fact that throughout the entire passage, the Suffering Servant is portrayed as a singular human personality. There is no hint of allegory or any clue that the Suffering Servant is to be taken allegorically as referring to Israel. He goes through all the functions that an individual personality goes through. There is no personification of Israel at all in this passage. Israel is kept distinct from the Suffering Servant. Messiah is being viewed as a future historical person that would accomplish the prophecy of Isaiah. Israel is the people looking on while this is happening. This is no personification of Israel—only the view of a future historical person.

The fourth clue lies in the fact that the Suffering Servant is presented in the passage as an innocent sufferer (verses 4-6,8*b*,9*b*). It is easy to see how this can be true of the Messiah but is impossible of Israel. Moses and the prophets never told Israel: You will suffer for being innocent; but rather: You will suffer for your sins unless you repent and conform to the revealed will of God. God punished Israel many times and in various ways, and it was always because of sins. Both the Babylonian Exile and the present day Dispersion were results, according to the prophets, of disobedience on the part of Israel to the revealed will of God. This is in sharp contrast with the Suffering Servant, who is portrayed as an innocent sufferer.

The fifth clue is the fact that the Suffering Servant is further portrayed as a voluntary, willing, and silent sufferer (verse 7). He willingly submits to the suffering he undergoes and voices no complaint as to the injustice done him. Furthermore, as he undergoes these sufferings that lead him to his death, he is silent. In Israel's history, the Jews have been oppressed, gone into captivity, exile, and finally into present-day dispersion. But none of these occurred on a voluntary basis on Israel's part. Israel has generally fought back, and these things fell on Israel only because she was defeated and Israel was never defeated willingly. But the Messiah would be a willing sufferer. Furthermore, reading through the literature of Jewish history, it can barely be said that Israel was a silent sufferer. Rather, during her sufferings, Israel has always cried out against the inhumanity of those who were perpetrating the sufferings of Israel. Israel has produced a long line of literature catologing her sufferings and complaints. The activities of the Jewish Defense League show that there is a violence directed against anti-Semites and a desire to see them destroyed. So this, too, rules out making the Suffering Servant the personification of Israel and again points to it as referring to the Messiah.

The sixth clue is that in this passage the Suffering Servant suffers a vicarious and substitutionary death (verses 4-6,8,10,12). He suffers for the sake of others, so that they need not suffer for their sins. Nowhere in the Scriptures or in Jewish history do we ever see Israel suffering for the Gentiles. Israel often suffers *because of* the Gentiles but never *for* the Gentiles. Israel suffers, but Israel always suffers for her own sins. There is no substitution where Israel is concerned, only where the Messiah is concerned.

The seventh clue that is given is that the sufferings of the Servant of Jehovah bring justification and spiritual healing to those who accept it (verses 5*b*, 11*b*). The sufferings of Israel have failed to bring justification and spiritual healing to the Gentiles. After three thousand years of Jewish suffering, the Gentiles are hardly justified and are still spiritually sick, as became obvious with the way that Gentile nations were involved in the Holocaust. But Messiah's suffering was to bring this justification and spiritual healing to Jewish lives, a point that will be further developed in the last chapter.

The eighth clue is a crucial one. The Suffering Servant dies (verses 8,12). The sufferings of the Servant lead to and end in death. This especially makes the personification of Israel in this passage impossible. The Jewish people are alive and well and have never been destroyed in spite of many attempts to destroy them by anti-Semites throughout the centuries. This again forces one to the conclusion that the Suffering Servant cannot be Israel personified but rather the individual personality of the Messiah. As for the people of Israel, they live.

The ninth and final clue naturally follows: the Suffering Servant is resurrected (verses 10-11). The one who died for sins does not stay dead but is resurrected and can see the results of his suffering in that he brings justification and spiritual healing to many. Since Israel never died, there is no need for a resurrection. But if a person like the Messiah dies, God will certainly resurrect him to live again.

This, then, is the conflict over Isaiah 53. If one simply reads the chapter as one would read any chapter of another book, no other conclusion can be reached than that the individual person spoken of is suffering for the sins of the Jewish people. And for centuries, this was the only conclusion that Judaism ever had—they labeled the Suffering Servant as the Messiah, the Son of Joseph. Later rabbinical interpretation which made the Suffering Servant a personification of Israel seemed more an attempt to explain *away* rather than an actual explanation of the passage. This chapter must be read without prejudice and taken simply for what it is saying. This chapter must not be interpreted in any way that is only a defense against Christian polemics, but only for what the content of the passage really is. The *traditional* Jewish viewpoint is most in harmony with the simple statements of the text itself, speaking of it as the sufferings of the Messiah for the sins of Israel.

3.
The Messiah of the Old Testament
Part 2

If the Old Testament only spoke of Messiah in terms of his suffering, it would hardly give us enough to go on. But there is much more to the Old Testament picture of the Messiah than that which is found in Isaiah 53. In these other passages there is often less conflict—if any at all—than the conflict over Isaiah 53. These other passages, taken along with Isaiah 53, go a long way to show how the Messiah was to be a thoroughly unique person.

The Uniqueness of His Birth

Following the account of the creation, the Old Testament continues with the story of Adam and Eve. Satan in the guise of a serpent deceives Eve and causes her to break the one commandment of God. Adam follows suit. The result is that sin enters the human family and the human experience. Man now stands under the righteous judgment of God. Nevertheless, at the time of the fall, God provides for future redemption. As he addresses Satan, God says: "And I will put enmity between thee and the woman, and between thy seed and her seed: he shall bruise thy head, and thou shalt bruise his heel" (Gen. 3:15).

The key note of this verse is the statement: seed of

the woman. In and of itself, this statement may not seem unusual, but in the context of biblical teaching, it is most unusual. For throughout the Hebrew Scriptures, a man's lineage was never reckoned after the woman but only after the man. In all the genealogies we have in the biblical record, women are virtually ignored because they are unimportant in determining genealogy. Yet the future person who would crush Satan's head while himself only suffering a slight wound would not be reckoned after a man but after a woman. In the biblical pattern, this is highly unusual.

In spite of the normal biblical pattern, we have a clear statement that the future redeemer comes from the seed of the woman. His birth will only take into account his mother. For a reason that is not explained here, the father will not be taken into an account at all. Yet this goes totally contrary to the whole biblical view regarding genealogies.

That this verse was taken to be messianic is clear from the *Targums of Jonathan* and the *Jerusalem Targums*. Furthermore, the Talmudic expression "Heels of the Messiah" seems to have been taken from this verse. But Genesis itself does not explain how or why this redeemer can be labeled "seed of the woman" when it goes contrary to the biblical pattern.

Centuries later, Israel had a great prophet in the person of Isaiah. It was left to this prophet to explain the meaning and reason why the Messiah would be only reckoned after the seed of the woman. Isaiah writes; "Therefore the Lord himself will give you a sign: behold a virgin shall conceive, and bear a son, and shall call his name Immanuel" (7:14).

The very fact that the birth of this person spoken of in this passage is described as a "sign" points to some unusual thing regarding the birth. In other words, the birth could not be normal, for that would not fulfill the requirement of the word "sign." It had to be unusual in some way, perhaps miraculous or at least attention-getting.

The very existence of the Jewish people stemmed from a "sign" of a birth. The Scriptures make clear that both Abraham and Sarah were beyond the point of being able to bear children. Abraham was ninety-nine years old and Sarah eighty-nine. She had, of course, already undergone menopause when in Genesis 18, God promised that Sarah would have a son within one year. This would be the "sign" that God will keep his covenant with Abraham and will make a great nation from him. A year later this "sign" took place in the birth of Isaac, through whom the Jewish people came. It was the sign needed to authenticate the covenant. This was a miraculous birth.

The birth of the son in Isaiah 7:14 was also to be a sign—to be unusual in some way. But this time the unusual nature of the birth was not going to be due to the great age of the mother. This would be a sign by virtue of the fact that this son would be born of a virgin.

Right at this point, another conflict often ensues. Rabbis today claim that the Hebrew word *ALMAH* does not mean "virgin" but "young woman." But what they fail to explain is how this would be used as a sign. A young woman giving birth to a baby is hardly unusual, in fact, it happens all the time! Often Rashi is the one quoted as showing that *ALMAH* means "young woman." It is true that Rashi interpreted Isaiah 7:14 to mean a young woman, perhaps for the same reason that he made Isaiah 53 refer to Israel and not to the Messiah. But this is not enough to prove that Rashi always made *ALMAH* to mean a young woman. This Hebrew word is also found in the Song of Solomon 1:3 and 6:8. In these passages Rashi makes *ALMAH* to mean "virgin"! So, regardless of how Rashi interpreted Isaiah 7:14, he elsewhere did use the word *ALMAH* to mean "virgin." Furthermore, Rashi admitted that many Jewish scholars of his day made Isaiah 7:14 to refer to a virgin. It can easily be seen that Rashi was trying to counteract Christian polemics with his interpretation of Isaiah 7:14 rather than being honest with the text itself. Also, as in the case of Isaiah 53, Rashi was again going contrary to popular Jewish interpretation.

A far more authoritative Jewish source than Rashi is the judgment of the seventy Jewish rabbis who translated the Greek version of the Old Testament, known as the Septuagint, about 250 B.C. These men lived far closer to the time of Isaiah than Rashi—by about thirteen hundred years—and were closer to the original usage of the word. These seventy rabbis all made *ALMAH* to read *parthenos,* which is the simple Greek word for "virgin."

Even if *ALMAH* is allowed to mean "young woman," it still must be admitted that the word can refer to a virginal young woman. It must not be ignored that this birth was to be a sign—an unusual birth. This is best seen if taken to mean a virgin birth.

This, then, is the explanation of the mystery of Genesis 3:15. Messiah would be reckoned after the seed of a woman because he would *not* have a father. Because of a virgin birth, he could only be traced through his mother and not his father. Thus, Isaiah 7:14 clarifies the meaning of Genesis 3:15: The Messiah will enter the world by means of the virgin birth.

The Place of His Birth

Not only was the means of Messiah's birth prophecied, but so was the place of his birth. This was done by the prophet Micah, a contemporary of Isaiah. In chapter 5 of his book, verse 2, we read: "But thou, Bethlehem Ephrathah, which art little to be among the thousands of Judah, out of thee shall one come forth unto me that is to be ruler in Israel; whose goings forth are from of old, from everlasting." Concerning this verse, there is far less disagreement among Orthodox rabbis, since they generally take this to mean that the Messiah will originate from Bethlehem. This is the view taken by *The Soncino Books of the Bible,* which is the Orthodox Jewish commentary on the Old Testament and which takes as its source some earlier Jewish commentaries.

His Lineage

Another point that is uncontested is that the Messiah would be a descendant of King David. From this comes the rabbinical ascription of the title, Messiah, the Son of David. Of the numerous passages that might be cited, we will limit ourselves to the following two, both from Isaiah:

And there shall come forth a shoot out of the stock of Jesse, and a branch out of his roots shall bear fruit (11:1).

And it shall come to pass in that day, that the root of Jesse, that standeth for an ensign of the peoples, unto him shall the nations seek; and his resting-place shall be glorious (11:10).

Jesse was the father of David, and thus these passages show that Messiah will come from the house of David. To this all Orthodox Judaism agrees. Other passages regarding this same point will be cited later in a different context.

The Sufferings of the Messiah

That the Messiah will suffer and die was something that all early rabbis agreed would be. They referred to the suffering Messiah as Messiah, the Son of Joseph, making him distinct from Messiah, the Son of David. The central passage from this view was Isaiah 53, which has already been discussed. Another passage dealing with the sufferings of the Messiah was Psalm 22:1-21:

My God, my God, why hast thou forsaken me? Why art thou so far from helping me, and from the words of my groaning? O my God, I cry in the daytime, but thou answerest not; and in the night season, and am not silent. But thou art holy, O thou that inhabitest the praises of Israel. Our fathers trusted, in thee: They trusted, and thou didst deliver them. They cried unto thee, and were delivered: They trusted in thee, and were not put to shame. But I am a worm, and no man; a reproach of men, and despised of the people. All they that see me laugh me to scorn: they shoot out the lip, they shake the head, saying, Commit thyself unto Jehovah; let him deliver him: let him rescue him, seeing he delighteth in him. But thou art he that took me out of the womb; Thou didst make me trust when I was upon my mother's breasts. I was cast upon thee from the womb; thou art my God since my mother bare me. Be not far from me; for trouble is near; for there is none to help. Many bulls have compassed me; strong bulls of Bashan have beset me round. They gape upon me with their mouth, as a ravening and roaring lion. I am poured out like water, and all my bones are out of joint: my heart is like wax; it is melted within me. My strength is dried up like a potsherd; and my tongue cleaveth to my jaws; and thou hast brought me into the dust of death. For dogs have compassed me: a company of evil-doers have inclosed me; they pierced my hands and my feet. I may count all my bones; they look and stare upon me. They part my garments among them, and upon my vesture do they cast lots. But be not thou far off, O Jehovah: O thou my succor, haste thee to help me. Deliver my soul from the sword, my darling from the power of the dog. Save me from the lion's mouth; yea, from the horns of the wild-oxen thou hast answered me.

To summarize the passage, we find that the Messiah is forsaken by God, is ridiculed and tormented by the people, and his clothes are gambled away by his tormentors. He suffers such agony that his bones all come out of joint, his heart breaks with a mixture of blood and water, and his hands and feet are all pierced. In many ways this psalm is very similar to Isaiah 53, providing even more detail as to the type of suffering and agony that the Messiah must undergo. The rabbis in the *Yalkut* also referred this passage to Messiah, the Son of Joseph.

Messiah the King of Israel

In all the passages discussed so far, Messiah was

portrayed as a man, but a man of sorrows. He was to suffer and die. The earlier rabbis all recognized this to speak of Messiah, and called him Messiah, the Son of Joseph. For as Joseph the patriarch suffered at the hands of his brethren, Messiah would too. But other passages spoke of another kind of Messiah, not a sufferer, but a conqueror, not a dying Messiah but a reigning one. This one was called Messiah, the Son of David by the rabbis. Most of what is said about the Messiah in Moses and the Prophets revolves around the Messiah coming to bring peace and to establish the messianic kingdom over Israel. There are far too many such passages to even begin to list here, but two such passages will be quoted in full. It should be noted how differently this Messiah is portrayed in comparison with all the previous passages thus far discussed. It is little wonder that the early rabbis were confused and so devised the theory of the two Messiahs, each coming once. The first passage is found in Isaiah 11:1-10:

And there shall come forth a shoot out of the stock of Jesse, and a branch out of his roots shall bear fruit. And the Spirit of Jehovah shall rest upon him, the spirit of wisdom and understanding, the spirit of counsel and might, the spirit of knowledge and of the fear of Jehovah. And his delight shall be in the fear of Jehovah; and he shall not judge after the sight of his eyes, neither decide after the hearing of his ears; but with righteousness shall he judge the poor, and decide with equity for the meek of the earth; and he shall smite the earth with the rod of his mouth, and with the breath of his lips shall he slay the wicked. And righteousness shall be the girdle of his waist, and faithfulness the girdle of his loins.

And the wolf shall dwell with the lamb, and the leopard shall lie down with the kid; and the calf and the young lion and the fatling together; and a little child shall lead them. And the cow and the bear shall feed; their young ones shall lie down together; and the lion shall eat straw like the ox. And the suckling child shall play on the hole of the asp, and the weaned child shall put his hand on the adder's den. They shall not hurt nor destroy in all my holy mountain; for the earth shall be full of the knowledge of Jehovah, as the waters cover the sea.

And it shall come to pass in that day, that the root of Jesse, that standeth for an ensign of the peoples, unto him shall the nations seek; and his resting-place shall be glorious.

That this speaks of the Messiah and the messianic age the rabbis, both ancient and modern, agree. Unlike the previous passages, there is no picture of a dying Messiah being rebuked and despised by his people. The picture we get here is of a reigning Messiah who brings peace and prosperity to the entire world. The peace extends down to the animal kingdom. The wicked are removed in judgment, and differences between the nations are settled by Messiah's authoritative word. The knowledge of the God of Israel spreads until it covers the entire world. The whole world has an intimate knowledge of the God who created the world, now that the reigning Messiah has brought peace and prosperity to it.

A second passage which gives the same picture is found in Psalm 72:1-19:

Give the king thy judgments, O God, and thy righteousness unto the king's son. He will judge thy people with righteousness, and thy poor with justice. The mountains shall bring peace to the people, and the hills, in righteousness. He will judge the poor of the people, he will save the children of the needy, and will break in pieces the oppressor. They shall fear thee while the sun endureth, and so long as the moon, throughout all generations. He will come down like rain upon the mown grass, as showers that water the earth. In his days shall the righteous flourish, and abundance of peace, till the moon be no more. He shall have dominion also from sea to sea, and from the River unto the ends of the earth. They that dwell in the wilderness shall bow before him; and his enemies shall lick the dust. The kings of Tarshish and of the isles shall render tribute: the kings of Sheba and Seba shall offer gifts. Yea, all kings shall fall down before him; all nations shall serve him. For he will deliver the needy when he crieth, and the poor, that hath no helper. He will have pity on the poor and needy, and the souls of the needy he will save. He will redeem their soul from oppression and violence; and precious will their blood be in his sight: and they shall live; and to him shall be given of the gold of Sheba: and men shall pray for him continually; they shall bless him all the day long. There shall be abundance of grain in the earth upon the top of the mountains; the fruit thereof shall shake like Lebanon: and they of the city shall flourish like grass of the earth. His name shall endure forever; his name shall be continued as long as the sun: and men shall be blessed in him; all nations shall call him happy. Blessed be Jehovah God, the God of Israel, who only doeth wondrous things: and blessed be his glorious name for ever; and let the whole earth be filled with his glory. Amen, and Amen.

This psalm is applied as speaking of the righteous reign of the Messiah in the *Talmud,* and the *Targums* make the first verse to read as follows: "Give the sentence of thy judgment to the King Messiah, and thy justice to the son of David the King."

The *Midrash* on the Psalms follows suit and connects this psalm with Isaiah 11:1, which was quoted previously. Furthermore, among the many differing names given to the Messiah by the rabbis of the *Talmud* was the name *Yinnon,* which was taken from the Hebrew rendering of verse 17 in this very psalm. So this passage also presents a different view of the Messiah from the others discussed earlier in this chapter and the previous one. This, then, is a two-fold picture presenting a major problem to anyone trying to formulate what the Old Testament has to say about the Messiah.

Other passages that deal with the kingship of the Messiah give us two other aspects of the person of the Messiah. One of these is the sonship of the Messiah with God, and the other involves the God-Man concept. In order to get a complete picture of the Old Testament's concept of the Messiah, it is necessary to discuss these two points, which we will touch on briefly.

Messiah's Sonship with God

Two passages make the point that the Messiah is also in some way the Son of God. The first of these is Psalm 2, which deals primarily with the kingship of the Messiah, but which also brings out the Messiah's sonship with God. The twelve verses of the psalm read as follows:

Why do the nations [Gentiles] rage, and the peoples meditate a vain thing? The kings of the earth set themselves, and the rulers take counsel together, against Jehovah, and against his anointed [Messiah], saying, Let us break their bonds asunder, and cast away their cords from us. He that sitteth in the heavens will laugh: the Lord will have them in derision. Then will he speak unto them in his wrath, and vex them in his sore displeasure: yet I have set my king upon my holy hill of Zion.

I will tell of the decree: Jehovah said unto me, Thou art my son; this day have I begotten thee. Ask of me, and I will give thee the nations for thine inheritance, and the uttermost parts of the earth for thy possession. Thou shalt break them with a rod of iron; thou shalt dash them in pieces like a potter's vessel.

Now therefore be wise, O ye kings: be instructed, ye judges of the earth. Serve Jehovah with fear, and rejoice with trembling. Kiss the son, lest he be angry, and ye perish in the way, for his wrath will soon be kindled. Blessed are all they that take refuge in him.

Concerning this psalm, Rashi admits, "Our rabbis expound it as relating to King Messiah." Although the majority of rabbis in earlier years also expounded this psalm as of King Messiah, many rabbis today would refer it to David rather than Messiah. But the words of the psalm and a comparison of history would exclude David as a possibility altogether. In this passage, God tells the person he is speaking to that he is turning over the dominion and the authority of the whole world to him. History makes very clear that David never had that dominion, nor was he ever able to exercise that authority. Hence, David must needs be excluded. Thus, the early rabbis were correct in interpreting this psalm to speak of the Messiah, who in this psalm is referred to as the Son of God.

Also in this same psalm, God warns that all must submit to the Son of God, the Messiah. Those who refuse will be punished. Those, however, who take refuge in the Messiah, that is, place their faith and trust in him for their salvation, will receive new life.

The second passage comes from the wise king, Solomon. In the book of Proverbs, in chapter 30, verse 4, we have a series of six questions. The first four questions all have the same question of identity: Who did it? Here they are. Number one: *"Who has gone up into heaven and come down?"* Number two: *"Who has gathered the wind in his fists?"* Number three: *"Who has bound up the waters in his garment?"* Number four: *"Who has established all the ends of the earth?"* These are four questions that Solomon is asking, indicating that the answer is very clear. When we look at the events described in these four questions, it is obvious that only one person could possibly do all those things: God himself.

Now we come to the fifth question: *"What is his name?"* We see that only God can do those things in the first four questions, but now, what is God's name? His name no one really knows how to pronounce anymore, for throughout the centuries we feared to take God's name in vain. So the pronunciation has been forgotten. In Hebrew we have it in the four letter *YHVH*. It is the name for which we substitute the word *Adonai*. In English we sometimes give it the name *Jehovah*. The name is *YHVH*, the great I AM. So it is God, the great I AM, who did all these things.

Now let us go on to the sixth and last question, which is found in the very same verse: *"What is his son's name, if you know?"* Notice how Solomon is posing the sixth question. We first had four questions asking who did all these great things. The answer was: God did all those things. The fifth question was: What is God's name?

The answer: *YHVH*, the great I AM is his name. But then Solomon poses a trick question because he knows at this stage of biblical history it would be impossible to answer. That is why he adds to the sixth question the phrase: *"If you know?"* The question is: *"What is his son's name, if you know?"* The obvious meaning here is that this God, the great I AM, has a son. Up to the time of Solomon and after, we did not know his name because it was not as yet revealed. This was not an unusual approach in the Scriptures. For instance, throughout the whole history of the book of Genesis, no one knew God's name because God first revealed it to Moses in the book of Exodus (3:14-15 6:2-3) The people living during the time of Genesis knew that there was a God, they just did not know his name. By the same token, no one knew the name of the Son of God throughout Old Testament Judaism. But Old Testament Judaism did know that God had a son, for both David and Solomon spoke of him.

The Messiah's sonship with God is thus related to his messiahship. In Psalm 2, this sonship is related strongly to Messiah's kingship.

The God-Man Concept and the Messiah

Another aspect involving the kingship of the Messiah is the strange God-Man concept concerning the Messiah. Some passages dealing with the kingship of the Messiah add a whole new dimension as to the person of the Messiah, making him a man and yet more than a man. One of these is Isaiah 9:6-7

For unto us a child is born, unto us a son is given; and the government shall be upon his shoulder: and his name shall be called Wonderful, Counsellor, Mighty God, Ever-lasting father, Prince of Peace. Of the increase of his government and of peace there shall be no end, upon the throne of David, and upon his kingdom, to establish it, and to uphold it with justice and with righteousness from henceforth even for ever. The zeal of Jehovah of hosts will perform this.

Verse 6 declares that a son is born into the Jewish world who will eventually control the reigns of government. Verse 7 identifies him as the Messianic descendant of David; it gives a dramatic description of his reign, which will be characterized by peace and justice. But in verse 6 he is given names that can only be true of God himself. "Wonderful Counsellor" and "Prince of Peace" can be true of a man, but "Mighty God" and "Everlasting Father" cannot. This new dimension presented by Isaiah regarding the person of the Messiah is that the Messiah had to be a man, a descendant of David, but also he was to be God as well.

This further explains what Isaiah had said two chapters earlier (Isa. 7:14) when he stated: "Therefore the Lord himself will give you a sign: behold, a virgin shall conceive, and bear a son, and shall call his name Immanuel."

In this passage, which we discussed earlier, Isaiah declares that there is going to be a son born of a virgin. Then he is given a name which is said to be *Immanuel.* In the Bible, when a parent names his child, it shows the thinking of the parents. However, when God gives a person a name, it actually represents his very character, as only God can foresee. So when this child is named by God *Immanuel,* the name portrays the actual character of the child. What does *Immanuel* mean? It means:

With Us, God. So here we have a child that is born of a virgin who is *With Us, God* or *God is among us!* The Isaiah 9 portion further clarifies that this son is a descendant of David, and he is labeled as God himself. So Isaiah clearly portrays the Messiah as the God-Man.

Nor is Isaiah alone in presenting this picture. Jeremiah echoes Isaiah in chapter 23, verses 5-6:

> Behold, the days come, saith Jehovah, that I will raise unto David a righteous Branch, and he shall reign as king and deal wisely, and shall execute justice and righteousness in the land. In his days Judah shall be saved, and Israel shall dwell safely; and this is his name whereby he shall be called: Jehovah our righteousness.

Here, too, a descendant of David reigns upon the throne of David, and the character of his reign is described as one of peace and security for Israel. Yet he is given the very name of God, which can only belong to God himself—*Adonai Tzidkenu*—Jehovah our righteousness. This is the *YHVH*, the very name God revealed to Moses as being his own personal name—I AM. So once again the future king Messiah of Israel is seen as a man on one hand but as God on the other. As with the sonship concept, the God-Man concept is related to Messiah's kingship.

This, then, concludes the picture given of the Messiah in the Old Testament. On the one hand he is a suffering and dying Messiah. On the other he is a conquering and reigning Messiah called God and the Son of God. The solution of the rabbis was to formulate the doctrine of two Messiahs: Messiah, the Son of Joseph, and Messiah, the Son of David.

But this is not the only option.

4.

What the New Testament Says About Jesus

The primary point of the New Testament is that Jesus is the Jewish Messiah of the Old Testament. While each of the four biographies on the life of Jesus that have come down to us have their own theme, they still all make one primary point: Jesus is the Messiah. The New Testament begins with the words: "The book of the genealogy of Jesus the Messiah the son of David, the son of Abraham." This opening statement of the New Testament sets the stage for the entire New Testament.

Messiahship—Kingship—Jewishness

Giving Jesus the title of Messiah points to his messiahship and has the Messiah spoken of in the Old Testament in mind. The word "Christ" is simply the Greek word for the word "Messiah."

Giving Jesus the title of the son of Abraham, points to the Jewishness of Jesus, since throughout biblical history and theology, Jewishness was always associated with the covenant God made with Abraham.

Giving Jesus the title of the son of David, points to his kingship, since the kingship of the Jews was sustained through the house of David.

The entire New Testament revolves around this opening statement. This statement will be repeated, developed, and enlarged upon by the various writers of the New Testament:

And to Jacob was born Joseph the husband of Miriam by whom was born Jesus, who is called Messiah. (Matt. 1:16). *(Messiahship.)*

The woman said unto him, I know that the Messiah is coming, and when he comes he will tell us all things. Jesus said to her, I who am speaking to you am he (John 4:25-26). *(Messiahship.)*

Now when Jesus was born in Bethlehem of Judah in the days of Herod the king, behold, Wise-men from the east came to Jerusalem saying: Where is he that is born king of the Jews? for we saw his star in the east and are come to worship him (Matt. 2:1-2). *(Kingship.)*

And they set up over his head his accusation written, This is Jesus the king of the Jews (Matt. 27:37). *(Kingship.)*

The Samaritan woman therefore saith unto him, How is it that thou, being a Jew askest drink of me, who am a Samaritan woman? (John 4:9). *(Jewishness.)*

But when the fulness of the time came, God sent forth his Son, born of a woman, born under the law, and that he might redeem them that were under the law, that we might receive the adoption of sons (Gal. 4:4-5). *(Jewishness.)*

For verily not to angels doth he give help, but he giveth help to the seed of Abraham (Heb. 2:16). *(Jewishness.)*

His messiahship, his kingship, and his Jewishness are the dominant claims of the New Testament. This is true of the Gospels, the four biographies of his life, as well as of the rest of the writings of the New Testament which deal with the theology of the life of Jesus. He is clearly portrayed as the Messiah of the Old Testament.

The Son of Joseph and the Son of David

Most of what the Gospels have to say place Jesus squarely into the mold of the Old Testament Messiah. He would be the one that the rabbis referred to as the Messiah, the Son of Joseph: "Philip findeth Nathanael, and saith unto him, We have found him, of whom Moses in the law, and the prophets, wrote, Jesus of Nazareth, the son of Joseph" (John 1:45).

But he is also portrayed by the four biographies as the very Messiah whom the rabbis referred to as being Messiah, the Son of David:

> . . . thou shalt call his name Jesus. He shall be great, and shall be called the Son of the Most High: and the Lord God shall give unto him the throne of his father David: and he shall reign over the house of Jacob for ever; and of his kingdom there shall be no end (Luke 1:31-33).

How could both aspects be true of the same person? The answer of the Talmudic rabbis, as we have already discussed, was to declare that it could not be. Hence, they adopted the two-Messiahs theory, making one the suffering Messiah and the other the conquering and reigning Messiah. The New Testament declares, however, that there is an alternative to the two-Messiahs view and goes on to show how the two aspects can indeed be true of the same person.

The Uniqueness of His Birth

First, as has already been stated, the primary point of the Gospels is to portray Jesus as the Messiah who came to suffer and die for sin. He was the one the rabbis would have called Messiah, the Son of Joseph. Jesus was the Messiah who came into the world in both a normal and a miraculous way: normal, in that he came into the world by birth, as do all other human beings; miraculous, in that he was given birth by a virgin:

And the angel said unto her, Fear not, Mary: for thou hast found favor with God. And behold, thou shalt conceive in thy womb, and bring forth a son, and shalt call his name Jesus. . . . And Mary said unto the angel, How shall this be, seeing I know not a man? And the angel answered and said unto her, The Holy Spirit shall come upon thee, and the power of the Most High shall overshadow thee: wherefore also the holy thing which is begotten shall be called the Son of God (Luke 1:30-31,34-35).

And she shall bring forth a son; and thou shalt call his name Jesus; for it is he that shall save his people from their sins. Now all this is come to pass, that it might be fulfilled which was spoken by the Lord through the prophet, saying, Behold, the virgin shall be with child, and shall bring forth a son, and they shall call his name Immanuel; which is, being interpreted, God with us (Matt. 1:21-23).

The virgin birth of the Messiah, first hinted at in Genesis 3:15 and later developed by Isaiah 7:14, is viewed by the Gospels as being fulfilled in the birth of Jesus.

His Davidic lineage is established by the fact that both Mary, his mother, and Joseph, his stepfather, were descendants of King David. So on his mother's side, Jesus was a descendant of David by blood and on his stepfather's side by adoption.

The Place of His Birth

Furthermore, his birthplace was in Bethlehem, although his parents lived in Nazareth:

> And all went to enrol themselves, every one to his own city. And Joseph also went up from Galilee, out of the city of Nazareth, into Judaea, to the city of David, which is called Bethlehem, because he was of the house and family of David; to enrol himself with Mary, who was betrothed to him, being great with child. And it came to pass, while they were there, the days were fulfilled that she should be delivered. And she brought forth her firstborn son; and she wrapped him in swaddling clothes, and laid him in a manger, because there was no room for them in the inn (Luke 2:3-7).

Thus, the birth of Christ is seen to be the fulfillment of Micah 5:2, which declared that the Messiah would be born in Bethlehem.

His Sufferings and Death

But more than anything else, the sufferings and death of Jesus fit the mold developed by Isaiah 53. Jesus is portrayed as the historical individual personality fulfilling to the letter the content of Isaiah 53. He was innocent of any sin and so suffered innocently: "Him who knew no sin he made to be sin on our behalf; that we might become the righteousness of God in him" (2 Cor. 5:21).

He was a voluntary sufferer and willingly allowed himself to be mistreated by those who took him captive: "I lay down my life, that I may take it again. No one taketh it away from me, but I lay it down of myself" (John 10:17-18).

Not only did he submit himself to the mistreatment resulting in suffering and death, but he did so silently, without any real protest. One of the very things that surprised and amazed men at his trial was his total

silence, never vocalizing protest against the injustice of
the false accusations:

> And when he was accused by the chief priests and elders, he
> answered nothing. Then saith Pilate unto him, Hearest thou
> not how many things they witness against thee? And he gave
> him no answer, not even to one word: insomuch that the
> governor marvelled greatly (Matt. 27:12-14).

All his sufferings, however, were vicarious, that is, he
was suffering for the sins of others rather than his own:

> For hereunto were ye called: because Christ also suffered for
> you, leaving you an example, that ye should follow his steps:
> who did no sin, neither was guile found in his mouth: who, when
> he was reviled, reviled not again; when he suffered, threatened
> not; but committed himself to him that judgeth righteously: who
> his own self bare our sins in his body upon the tree, that we,
> having died unto sins, might live unto righteousness; by whose
> stripes ye were healed (1 Pet. 2:21-24).

The death of Jesus is seen by the New Testament
writers to be the fulfillment of all the factors regarding
the death of the Suffering Servant in Isaiah 53. Just as
the suffering of the Suffering Servant ended in death,
after scourgings, mockery, and crucifixion, so Jesus dies.
Just as the Suffering Servant is treated as a criminal and
dies a criminal's death, so Jesus, by dying a death by
means of crucifixion, died a criminal's death along with
two other criminals. The death of the Suffering Servant
was a result of a judicial sentencing and a judicial
judgment. Jesus underwent two trials, the first a religious
one in which he was condemned on false charges of
blasphemy and sentenced to death; the second, later,

a political trial by the Romans on false charges of fomenting rebellion against Caesar. Again he was sentenced to death and underwent this Roman type of tortuous death. Although, like the Suffering Servant, he was assigned a criminal's grave, he nevertheless was buried in a rich man's tomb:

And when even was come, there came a rich man from Arimathea, named Joseph, who also himself was Jesus' disciple: this man went to Pilate, and asked for the body of Jesus. Then Pilate commanded it to be given up. And Joseph took the body, and wrapped it in a clean linen cloth, and laid it in his own new tomb, which he had hewn out in the rock: and he rolled a great stone to the door of the tomb, and departed (Matt. 27:57-60). ✗

In the Isaiah passage, the Suffering Servant does not stay dead but is resurrected to see the results of his sufferings and death. Three days after the body of Jesus is buried in a rich man's tomb, his death gives away to resurrection. Finally, the Gospels record that forty days after the resurrection, Jesus ascended into heaven and now sits at the right hand of God, just as the Suffering Servant was to be "exalted and lifted up, and . . . be very high" (Isa. 52:13). ✗

Finally, the Isaiah passage concluded that the Suffering Servant would bring justification and spiritual healing to those who would accept his substitutionary death on their behalf. He would bring justification, redemption, and reconciliation to many. Whether or not Jesus has done this will be discussed in the last chapter.

Not only is the life of Jesus portrayed as fitting the ✗ mold of Isaiah 53, but it is also portrayed as fitting the mold of Psalm 22. While dying on the cross, Jesus cries out the first verse of the psalm, "My God, my God, why hast thou forsaken me?" (Matt. 27:46). The Roman soldiers gambled for his clothes:

> And when they had crucified him, they parted his garments among them, casting lots (Matt. 27:35).

> The soldiers therefore, when they had crucified Jesus, took his garments and made four parts, to every soldier a part; and also the coat: now the coat was without seam, woven from the top throughout. They said therefore one to another, Let us not rend it, but cast lots for it, whose it shall be: that the scripture might be fulfilled, which saith, They parted my garments among them, and upon my vesture did they cast lots (John 19:23-24).

While Jesus hangs on the cross, the people ridicule him, using almost the very same words found in Psalm 22:8: "He trusteth on God; let him deliver him now, if he desireth him: for he said, I am the Son of God." (Matt. 27:43).

As in Psalm 22, when his side is pierced by a spear, a mixture of blood and water pours out which is the sign of a broken heart. Finally, his hands and feet having been nailed on the cross, they are pierced just as the person in Psalm 22 is pierced.

Thus, the Jesus of the New Testament is portrayed as the Messiah of the Old Testament with regard to his suffering and death. In all, Jesus fulfilled about three hundred prophecies dealing with the coming of the Messiah by his life, suffering, death, and resurrection. Jesus fulfills, according to the New Testament, all that the rabbis expected of the Messiah the Son of Joseph.

The New Testament Solution to the Paradox

But what about the prophecies dealing with the Messiah as a king? What about his coming to restore peace and prosperity on the earth? What about the messianic figure that the rabbis termed Messiah, the Son of David? While the rabbis sought to solve the paradox by developing the two-Messiahs concept, the New Testament offers a different alternative. Instead of Two Messiahs, each coming one time, the New Testament speaks of one Messiah coming two times. He first comes by birth to the world, lives his life on the earth, eventually undergoing a period of suffering which ends in death for the sins of Israel. He is then resurrected and returns to his place in heaven. At some future time he will return to set up the messianic kingdom by reestablishing the Davidic throne and will reign over a kingdom of peace, prosperity, and security for Israel. But in the meantime, anyone who will believe and accept the substitutionary death for his sins will be justified and reconciled with God and have a living relationship with the God of Abraham, Isaac, and Jacob.

A number of passages in the New Testament speak of one Messiah coming two times. After the death and resurrection of Jesus, the New Testament looks forward to his return to set up the kingdom. Of these numerous passages, we will quote only the following few:

Jesus said unto them, Verily I say unto you, that ye who have followed me, in the regeneration when the Son of man shall sit on the throne of his glory, ye also shall sit upon twelve thrones, judging the twelve tribes of Israel (Matt. 19:28).

But immediately after the tribulation of those days the sun shall be darkened, and the moon shall not give her light, and the stars shall fall from heaven, and the powers of the heavens shall be shaken: and then shall appear the sign of the Son of man in heaven: and then shall all the tribes of the earth mourn, and they shall see the Son of man coming on the clouds of heaven with power and great glory. And he shall send forth his angels with a great sound of a trumpet, and they shall gather together his elect from the four winds, from one end of heaven to the other (Matt. 24:29-31).

But when the Son of man shall come in his glory, and all the angels with him, then shall he sit on the throne of his glory (Matt. 25:31).

He shall be great, and shall be called the Son of the Most High: and the Lord God shall give unto him the throne of his father David: and he shall reign over the house of Jacob for ever; and of his kingdom there shall be no end (Luke 1:32-33).

They therefore, when they were come together, asked him, saying, Lord, dost thou at this time restore the kingdom to Israel? And he said unto them, It is not for you to know times or seasons, which the Father hath set within his own authority (Acts 1:6-7).

For I would not, brethren, have you ignorant of this mystery, lest ye be wise in your own conceits, that a hardening in part hath befallen Israel, until the fulness of the Gentiles be come in; and so all Israel shall be saved: even as it is written, There shall come out of Zion the Deliverer; he shall turn away ungodliness from Jacob: and this is my covenant unto them, when I shall take away their sins (Rom. 11:25-27).

But now hath Christ been raised from the dead, the first-fruits of them that are asleep. For since by man came death, by man came also the resurrection of the dead. For as in Adam all die, so also in Christ shall all be made alive. But each in his own order: Christ the firstfruits; then they that are Christ's, at his coming. Then cometh the end, when he shall deliver up the kingdom to God, even the Father; when he shall have abolished all rule and all authority and power. For he must reign, till he hath put all his enemies under his feet. The last enemy that shall be abolished is death. For, He put all things in subjection under his feet. But when he saith, All things are put in subjection, it is evident that he is excepted who did subject all things unto him. And when all things have been subjected unto him, then shall the Son also himself be subjected to him that did subject all things to him, that God may be all in all (1 Cor. 15:20-28).

And inasmuch as it is appointed unto men once to die, and after this cometh judgment; so Christ also, having been once offered to bear the sins of many, shall appear a second time, apart from sin, to them that wait for him, unto salvation (Heb. 9:27-28).

And I saw thrones, and they sat upon them, and judgment was given unto them: and I saw the souls of them that had been beheaded for the testimony of Jesus, and for the word of God, . . . and they lived, and reigned with Christ a thousand years. The rest of the dead lived not until the thousand years should be finished. This is the first resurrection. Blessed and holy is he that hath part in the first resurrection: over these the second death hath no power; but they shall be priests of God and of Christ, and shall reign with him a thousand years (Rev. 20:4-6).

All these verses indicate that Jesus is to come again and establish the kingdom. Connected with the kingship passages in the Old Testament were also the Sonship of the Messiah with God and the God-Man concepts. Both of these ideas are also to be found in the quotations just given from the New Testament regarding Christ.

The God-Man Concept and Jesus

Another factor regarding the Messiah in Isaiah 9:6-7 and Jeremiah 23:5-6 was the God-Man concept. In other words, Messiah was to be both man and God at the same time. Does the New Testament teach the same thing about Jesus? In the New Testament book of Philippians, chapter 2, verses 5-8 we read:

Have this mind in you, which was also in Christ Jesus: who, existing in the form of God, counted not the being on an equality with God a thing to be grasped, but emptied himself, taking the form of a servant, being made in the likeness of men; and being found in fashion as a man, he humbled himself, becoming obedient even unto death, yea, the death of the cross.

Furthermore, in the New Testament book of John, chapter 1, verses 1-2,14 we read: "In the beginning was the Word, and the Word was with God, and the Word was God. The same was in the beginning with God. . . . And the Word became flesh, and dwelt among us."

The Sonship of Jesus with God

Again, the Jewish writers of the New Testament see in Jesus the messianic requirements of the Old Testament right down to the God-Man concept. Now only one thing remains. Does the New Testament make Jesus the Son of God as demanded by Psalm 2 and Proverbs 30:4? Going back to Luke chapter 1, where Gabriel announces to Mary the virgin the coming miraculous birth of the Messiah, we read in verses 34-35:

And Mary said unto the angel, How shall this be, seeing I know not a man? And the angel answered and said unto her, The Holy Spirit shall come upon thee and the power of the Most High shall overshadow thee: wherefore also the holy thing which is begotten shall be called the Son of God.

According to this passage Messiah Jesus would be called the Son of God because of his miraculous conception and virgin birth. In every way this is in keeping with the demands of the Old Testament. Years later, when Jesus is about to begin his career of public ministry, we read in Matthew chapter 3, verses 16-17:

And Jesus, when he was baptized, went up straightway from the water: and lo, the heavens were opened unto him, and he saw the Spirit of God descending as a dove, and coming upon him; and lo, a voice out of the heavens, saying, This is my beloved Son, in whom I am well pleased.

Conclusion

To conclude this discussion on what the New Testament says about Jesus, it proclaims him to be the Messiah of the Old Testament. The New Testament solution to the Old Testament paradox is that there will only be one Messiah, and this Messiah would come two times. This seems to be consistent with the Old Testament, since often the Old Testament passages speak of the suffering and the conquering aspects of the Messiah in one and the same passage, giving no indication at all that two persons are meant.

But if all this is true, why do so many Jewish people not believe in Jesus? Why do Jews object to the messiahship of Jesus? The next chapters will deal with some of these questions.

5.
Why Did the Messiah Have to Die?

Because the whole concept of a dying Messiah is so foreign to modern Judaism, although once it was part of Judaism, there is a question which must be answered: Why did the Messiah have to die? In the course of answering this question, a second one arises: What is the means of redemption?

If there is one theme that seems to go throughout the entire Scriptures, it is the theme of redemption by blood.

According to the Old Testament

Redemption became necessary when sin entered the human sphere and separated man from God. When Adam and Eve committed the first act of disobedience, sin entered and separated them from God. From that point on, the means of bridging the separation of man from God was the means of blood. This bridging of the gap is called redemption. In the history of God dealing with his people, the means of redemption was always by blood.

The redemptive element of blood begins to come into the theme of Scripture at the same time that sin does, for until sin came, no blood was necessary. We read that just as soon as man is expelled from the Garden

of Eden: "Jehovah God made for Adam and for his
wife coats of skins, and clothed them (Gen. 3:21).

The skins were animal skins. The nakedness that the
element of sin now revealed needed to be covered. But
the covering required the death of several animals and
so, for the first time in history, blood was shed. This
provides the root meaning of the Hebrew word for
atonement, which is "a covering."

The necessity of blood was a lesson soon learned by
the sons of the first human couple. The time came for
both Abel and Cain to bring their sacrifices before God.
Cain offered for sacrifice the fruit of his labors in the
field. The offering was vegetable, and it was bloodless.
Abel brought a blood offering taken from his flock.
When God passed judgment on the two types of offer-
ings, that of Cain was rejected and that of Abel was
accepted. So a lesson was taught: One cannot approach
God by whatever means one chooses. It is man who
sinned and offended the holy God; it is God who must
do the forgiving. Therefore, it is not for man to choose
the means of forgiveness but for God, and God has
chosen the means to be blood. Cain had chosen to
approach God in his own way, but he was rejected.
Abel chose the way God demanded and was accepted.

As biblical history develops in the book of Genesis,
we find that all the ones with whom God was pleased
come to him by means of blood. Noah immediately
offered up blood sacrifices when he left the ark. He
was followed by other great men in Jewish history—Abraham, Isaac, Jacob—all of whom were careful
to approach God by means of blood.

When Moses received the Law at Mount Sinai, the

redemptive element of blood ran through the entire Law with its 613 commandments. A great summary statement for the entire Law was to be found in the third book of Moses, Leviticus 17:11: "For the life of the flesh is in the blood; and I have given it to you upon the altar to make atonement for your souls: for it is the blood that maketh atonement by reason of the life."

It can easily be said that all of the Law revolves around this one statement. There are commandments which God gave in the Law that were to be obeyed. Disobedience was sin. If disobedience did take place, the means of atonement for the sin was blood. The book of Leviticus opens by giving great detail to the different types of blood sacrifices. All these different sacrifices had the same purpose: that the Jew might be rightly related to God. All seven feasts of Israel—Passover, Unleavened Bread, Firstfruits, Pentecost, Trumpets, Day of Atonement, and Tabernacles—required the shedding of blood. The Yom Kippur ceremony was greatly detailed in Leviticus 16, where careful instructions are given for the shedding of blood to atone for the sins of the Jewish nation. The tabernacle and the Temple both were built to expedite and to make efficient the required shedding of blood for the atonement of the people's sins. The holy of holies, which contained the Shekinah Glory, the visible manifestation of the presence of God, could only be entered once a year by only one man, the high priest. In order for him to enter, he had to have the blood of the Yom Kippur sacrifice with him, and this blood had to be sprinkled on the ark of the covenant, which contained the tablets of the Law itself:

Then shall he kill the goat of the sin-offering, that is for
the people, and bring his blood within the veil, and do with
his blood as he did with the blood of the bullock, and sprinkle
it upon the mercy-seat, and before the mercy-seat: and he
shall make atonement for the holy place, because of the
uncleannesses of the children of Israel, and because of their
transgressions, even all their sins: and so shall he do for the
tent of meeting, that dwelleth with them in the midst of their
uncleannesses. And there shall be no man in the tent of
meeting when he goeth in to make atonement in the holy
place, until he come out, and have made atonement for
himself, and for his household, and for all the assembly of
Israel (Lev. 16:15-17).

And so the principle stood throughout the remainder
of Old Testament history. But it was a burden to the
individual. These blood sacrifices had to be repeated
year in and year out, and they had to be done in the
Temple at Jerusalem. For the Jews living elsewhere in
the country miles from Jerusalem, it was a burden to
come every year to offer their sacrifices to the Lord
for the atonement of their sins. Only the faithful few,
those whom the prophets referred to as the *Remnant,*
loved God and his Law enough to do so in spite of
the burden it created. Others built their own altars on
mountains and hills closer to home and offered their
sacrifices there. But no atonement was granted at these
rival altars, and the prophets of God railed against and
condemned this deviation from the Law of God. Many
had failed to learn the lesson of Cain, that one cannot
come to God for forgiveness in any way one may choose
but one must come in the way God himself has chosen.

It was Isaiah the prophet who first provided the hope

that the day would come when the yearly burden will be lifted. In Isaiah 53 God declared that the Suffering Servant, the Messiah, would be the sacrifice for sin:

Yet it pleased Jehovah to bruise him; he hath put him to grief: when thou shalt make his soul an offering for sin, he shall see his seed, he shall prolong his days, and the pleasure of Jehovah shall prosper in his hand. He shall see of the travail of his soul, and shall be satisfied: by the knowledge of himself shall my righteous servant justify many; and he shall bear their iniquities (Isa. 53:10-11).

This, then, was the reason that Messiah had to die: to provide the blood sacrifice for sin once and for all. No longer would the Jews be burdened with the yearly and repeated sacrifices. All a person would need to do is to accept the Messiah's death on his behalf and his sins would be forgiven. Messiah had to die to provide that atonement, for blood was the means of redemption.

According to the New Testament

The book of Hebrews in the New Testament is the counterpart of the book of Leviticus in the Old Testament. To understand Hebrews one must first understand Leviticus. Just as Leviticus had a central verse in 17:11 around which the entire book and the Law revolved, the book of Hebrews also makes the very same point in its central verse, 9:22: "And according to the law, I may almost say, all things are cleansed with blood, and apart from shedding of blood there is no remission."

The book of Hebrews was written by a Hebrew Christian to a group of Hebrew Christian assemblies in Israel. It picks up the theme of Leviticus and the prophecy of Isaiah to show the superiority of the sacrifice of the Messiah. A number of passages bring these things out. One such passage is Hebrews 2:16-18:

For verily not to angels doth he give help, but he giveth help to the seed of Abraham. Wherefore it behooved him in all things to be made like unto his brethren, that he might become a merciful and faithful high priest in things pertaining to God, to make propitiation for the sins of the people. For in that he himself hath suffered being tempted, he is able to succor them that are tempted.

This passage makes the point that Messiah came as a Jew and underwent all the problems that a Jew had to go through in order that he might become a merciful and sympathetic high priest.

Another central passage is Hebrews 4:14-15:

Having then a great high priest, who hath passed through the heavens, Jesus the Son of God, let us hold fast our confession. For we have not a high priest that cannot be touched with the feeling of our infirmities; but one that hath been in all points tempted like as we are, yet without sin.

This passage develops further the very same point that Jesus is the sympathetic high priest, for he understands what an individual person has to undergo—he himself underwent all these things.

Another passage is Hebrews 7:22-25:

By so much also hath Jesus become the surety of a better covenant. And they indeed have been made priests many in number, because that by death they are hindered from continuing: but he, because he abideth for ever, hath his priesthood unchangeable. Wherefore also he is able to save to the uttermost them that draw near unto God through him, seeing he ever liveth to make intercession for them.

The superiority of the priesthood of Christ is pointed out by the fact of the mortality of all other priests. One high priest would serve, but sooner or later he would die; a new priest would need to be chosen to begin the cycle all over again. The life-and-death cycle proved to be a disadvantage to the old priesthood. The superiority of the priesthood of Christ is shown in that it abides eternally. For Jesus was resurrected, and by virtue of that resurrection, Jesus remains a high priest forever.

Another shortcoming of the Levitical system of priesthood is found in Hebrews 7:26-27:

> For such a high priest became us, holy, guileless, undefiled, separated from sinners, and made higher than the heavens; who needeth not daily, like those high priests, to offer up sacrifices, first for his own sins, and then for the sins of the people: for this he did once for all, when he offered up himself.

This passage indicates that the sacrifices had to be repeated day in and day out, year in and year out. The Messiah was to be the once-for-all sacrifice for sin. This is what happened when Jesus came and offered up his own blood as the atonement for sin. Also, in the old order of priesthood, the high priest had to sacrifice and shed blood for his own sins first before he could sacrifice and shed blood to make atonement for the sins of the people. Since Jesus was sinless, he did not need to first atone for his own sins, but with his own blood made atonement for all who would accept it.

Again, the superiority of the sacrifice of Christ as over against all other sacrifices is pointed out in Hebrews

9:11-15:

> But Christ having come a high priest of the good things
> to come, through the greater and more perfect tabernacle,
> not made with hands, that is to say, not of this creation, nor
> yet through the blood of goats and calves, but through his
> own blood, entered in once for all into the holy place, having
> obtained eternal redemption. For if the blood of goats and
> bulls, and the ashes of a heifer sprinkling them that have
> been defiled, sanctify unto the cleanness of the flesh: how
> much more shall the blood of Christ, who through the eternal
> Spirit offered himself without blemish unto God, cleanse your
> conscience from dead works to serve the living God? And
> for this cause he is the mediator of a new covenant, that a
> death having taken place for the redemption of the trans-
> gressions that were under the first covenant, they that have
> been called may receive the promise of the eternal inheritance.

Unlike the animal sacrifices, the sacrifice of Jesus
was to bring eternal redemption rather than temporary
atonement. Furthermore, even after the animal sacrifice,
the Jew was still conscious of his sins. Faith in the
sacrifice of Jesus, however, brings a complete cleansing
of the conscience of sins.

Another passage is found in Hebrews 9:28: "So Christ
also, having been once offered to bear the sins of many,
shall appear a second time, apart from sin, to them that
wait for him, unto salvation."

Here the two-fold aspect of Messiah's career is pointed
out. Jesus first came to be the sin offering for the people,
just as the Suffering Servant of Isaiah 53 needed to
be. Also, just as the Suffering Servant was the one who
bore the sins of many, Jesus did so through his death.
Now, the verse states that Jesus will come a second time

for a different purpose. The purpose of the first coming was to die for sin. The purpose of the second coming will be to establish the messianic kingdom.

Once again a contrast is drawn between the animal sacrifices and the blood sacrifice of Jesus in Hebrews 10:1-4:

> For the law having a shadow of the good things to come, not the very image of the things, can never with the same sacrifices year by year, which they offer continually, make perfect them that draw nigh. Else would they not have ceased to be offered? because the worshippers, having been once cleansed, would have had no more consciousness of sins. But in those sacrifices there is a remembrance made of sins year by year. For it is impossible that the blood of bulls and goats should take away sins.

The animal sacrifices had to be repeated year in and year out. While these sacrifices provided temporary atonement, they never provided permanent forgiveness of sins. Rather, the yearly sacrifices served to remind the Jewish person of his sins; he knew he would have to bring another sacrifice the next year as well. The consciousness of sins was still there. But the sacrifice of Jesus was once and for all and never needed to be repeated. Acceptance of the sacrifice of Jesus does not bring temporary atonement but permanent forgiveness. By accepting the substitutionary death of Jesus for his sins, one is not continually reminded of those sins, but one receives a complete cleansing. That is why the sacrifice of Jesus is so superior to the animal sacrifices of the old system.

The last passage is found in Hebrews 10:10-14:

By which will we have been sanctified through the offering of the body of Jesus Christ once for all. And every priest indeed standeth day by day ministering and offering oftentimes the same sacrifices, the which can never take away sins: but he, when he had offered one sacrifice for sins for ever, sat down on the right hand of God; henceforth expecting till his enemies be made the footstool of his feet. For by one offering he hath perfected for ever them that are sanctified.

This passage again points out how the high priest had to sacrifice day in and day out, and his work was never done. The high priest is viewed as standing to indicate this unfinished ministry. But Jesus, who offered himself as a sacrifice once and for all, is viewed as sitting at the right hand of God, thus showing that his work is complete. Furthermore, the animal sacrifices provided a yearly atonement but never permanently took away sins. But those who accept the sacrifice of Jesus are perfected forever; their sins are permanently removed.

Conclusion

The conclusion of both the Old and the New Testaments is that the means of redemption was by blood, and the permanent blood sacrifice was to be the Messiah himself. That is why the Messiah *had to die* according to the Old Testament. That is why Jesus *did die* according to the New Testament. Who killed Jesus was never the issue as far as the New Testament was concerned, for the Messiah *had to die*. It only became an issue years later because of anti-Semites seeking excuses to persecute the Jews. The only issue in the New Testament itself is whether one will accept the substitutionary sacrifice of Jesus for himself or not.

6.
Jewish Objections to Jesus

The more recent articles written by rabbis stating their objections to Jesus all judge him on the basis of his conformity, or lack of it, to modern Judaism. The articles written by Rabbi Milton Steinberg and Trude Weis-Rosmarin, who were quoted in the first chapter, are cases in point.

Jesus is all too often judged by twentieth-century Judaism rather than first-century Judaism or biblical Judaism. The question, however, can never be, Is Jesus the Messiah in accordance with Judaism today? Judaism today is too fragmented with messianic views ranging from "He will come" to "What Messiah! There will be no Messiah." The fact is that most Jews today do not believe in any Messiah at all. The real issue is, Is Jesus the Messiah of Old Testament Judaism?

Judaism today is far different from the Judaism of the Old Testament or even the Judaism of Jesus' day. Modern Judaism is certainly not the "father of Christianity." At best it is its brother, with biblical Judaism being the father of both. If one were to read the books of the Old Testament and compare their teachings with the Judaism of today, one could almost conclude that modern Judaism is a completely new religion! Certainly there are similarities between Judaism then and now.

Yet similarities exist between various religions and they are, nevertheless, distinct one from another. The real issue is whether Jesus is the Messiah of the Old Testament. The messiahship of Jesus must stand or fall on no other criterion than his fulfillment of the messianic prophecies of the Scriptures.

What Kind of God Do You Have?

Some Jewish objections to the messiahship of Jesus rest on questioning the virgin birth and Jesus' resurrection from the dead. Objections to these two matters are, however, not the real issue in themselves. The real issue is what kind of God one believes in. The question is not, Is such a thing as the virgin birth possible? Or, Is such a thing as resurrection from death possible? From the strictly human viewpoint they are not. The real question is, Can God do such things? If he cannot, he is not much of a God. But if God is God, and all that this particular title infers, includes, and indicates, he can do anything he wants to do. The only possible limits to God are the limits he places on himself.

If God is all powerful, things like the virgin birth and the resurrection are easy things for him to accomplish. It is an amazing inconsistency to allow that God has created the heavens and the earth and then to doubt his ability to bring about a virgin birth. If he can create the wonder and vastness of the universe and all the complexity of the single cell, the virgin birth and the resurrection are very simple matters. For a Jew who believes in God, there is no reason to doubt the miracle of the virgin birth. The real question is, Did it happen with the birth of Jesus? The Old Testament said that it *would* happen with the Messiah. The New Testament said that it *did* happen with Jesus.

Jesus Didn't Bring Peace, Did He?

The most common objection one hears to the messiahship of Jesus is this: He could not be the Messiah since he did not bring peace. Well, since he was not accepted, he could not very well bring peace, could he? Furthermore, the purpose of the Messiah's first coming, or as the early rabbis would have it, the purpose of the coming of the first Messiah, the Messiah, the Son of Joseph, was not to bring peace but to suffer and die. Peace would come through the coming of the second Messiah, the Messiah, the Son of David, or as the New Testament would have it, by the second coming of the Messiah. So the messiahship of Jesus must first be judged on whether he did suffer and die for sin, and then on whether those who believed in him received their justification and forgiveness of sins. That he suffered and died for the sins of Israel is the testimony of the eyewitness accounts we have in the New Testament. That Jews have been receiving and experiencing the forgiveness of their sins through faith in the substitutionary death of Jesus has been testified by many. Some Hebrew Christian testimonies will be shared in Chapter 8. Both Talmudic Judaism and the New Testament agree that there would be one coming of a Messiah to suffer and die, which would precede the coming of the Messiah to bring peace. The point of difference is the former's claim of two different Messiahs, and the latter's claim of one and the same person, Jesus.

So while it is true that Jesus did not bring peace,

that was not the purpose of Messiah's first coming. So this is not a valid argument against his messiahship. For Jesus will yet come again and will yet bring peace.

Christians Hate the Jews

Another objection to the messiahship of Jesus is not so much an objection against Jesus himself as it is against the way his name has been used throughout Jewish history. For have not Christians persecuted and killed Jews for centuries? Has not the cross been a symbol of death to Jews? Has not the church issued discriminatory laws against the Jews? Has not the name of Jesus been used to scorch Jewish homes and bodies? Has not baptism been used in forced conversions to Christianity and as an excuse to separate Jewish children from their families? All of this is true and so is a lot more. It may be questioned whether those who perpetrated these atrocities were really Christians, but they certainly called themselves that.

But is all that a valid argument against the messiahship of Jesus himself? Can Jesus be held responsible for the way in which his name has been used or misused by those who profess to follow him?

In the post-Maccabean period, a man by the name of John Hyrcanus became the ruler of Israel. Israel at that time was fighting for independence from those who would take it from her, such as the Hellenistic Syrians. Among John Hyrcanus' many acts of war was forcing people to convert to Judaism—if they did not, they were killed. When he captured the Greek cities, the residents were given the choice of converting to Judaism or dying by the sword. The entire Edomite nation (then known as the Idumeans) were forcefully converted to Judaism; many who refused died by the sword. Many acts of atrocity were thus committed in the name of Judaism.

Now suppose that many of those who lost their families and loved ones by these tactics began going on an all out campaign against Moses, whom they would consider the founder of Judaism. Suppose, because of all these acts of forced conversion and death, the Greeks and Edomites rejected all that Moses had to say. Suppose that Judaism would be rejected because of the horrible things perpetrated in its name. This would all be unfair, for just because John Hyrcanus used the name of Moses and killed in the name of Judaism did not mean that Moses or Judaism itself taught that such things ought to be done. Indeed, it would be very unfair to reject Judaism strictly on the grounds of the way some used the name of Judaism to accomplish their own desire.

By the same token, it would be very wrong to reject the messiahship of Jesus strictly on the grounds of the way some have used his name. For Jesus and the New Testament do not sanction such acts against the Jews. The New Testament, which taught the Gentiles that "salvation is of the Jews," forbade the persecution of the Jews. So if some who erroneously called themselves Christians used the name of Jesus for their own selfish war against the Jews, it still did not make it a Christ-like action. For if the Jesus of the New Testament is the true Jesus, such actions are as foreign to his character as could be possible. Hence, the messiahship of Jesus must be based on who he claimed to be. Does he fit the mold of the Messiah of the Old Testament? He must be accepted or rejected on this ground alone, not by teachings that were clouded or perverted by those who sought a pretense to persecute the Jews.

Theological Objections

Theological objections to Jesus by rabbinical authorities have so repeatedly attacked the same areas as to become stereotypical. These will usually center on the question of the virgin birth, the claim of Jesus to be Son of God, and the fact that Jews cannot believe that a man can become God. Objections to the virgin birth have already been dealt with in this chapter. The kind of God one believes in is still an issue.

As to the claim of Jesus to be the Son of God, one objection reads like this:

> The New Testament knows Jesus as the son of God and as Messiah. Judaism, however, does not acknowledge a son of God who was set apart and elevated above other human beings. The Jewish conviction is that all men are equal before God and no mortal can claim divinity.

Here is an example of how the messiahship of Jesus is judged purely on the basis of modern Judaism. Jesus could not be the Messiah, the writer says, since Judaism does not acknowledge a Son of God to begin with. The writer would have been more honest had he said that Judaism as he knows it, which is only modern Judaism, does not acknowledge a Son of God. (In the case of Reform Judaism, there would be no Messiah to begin with.) The writer effectively ignores centuries of Jewish theological treatments that certainly do treat the Messiah as being a Son of God. Had the writer taken the time to look at the early rabbinical interpretations of Psalm

2, it would have shown him not to make such a rash statement, which even Rashi did not do. The details of this question have been discussed in earlier pages. The question is whether Jesus is the Messiah of the Old Testament—not whether he is the Messiah of modern Judaism.

And of course, Jews cannot believe that any man could become God and that is why Jews cannot accept Jesus, say the rabbis. To begin with, the fact that a man cannot become God is very true, and no man can claim divinity. This is where modern Judaism has misconstrued the teachings of the New Testament. The New Testament never claimed that Jesus was a man who became God. This is heresy. This goes contrary to Judaism of any form: biblical, rabbinical or otherwise, and it also goes contrary to the Christian faith. Neither the New Testament nor Jesus ever taught that there was a man who became God.

The New Testament claims the reverse: It was God who became a man in the person of Jesus of Nazareth. If God became a man, this man would certainly be superior to other men. He would now be the God-Man. Certainly Judaism does not dare claim that God cannot become a man if he wanted to. The God of biblical Judaism is all powerful. God can do anything he wants to. If there is anything God cannot do, he is less than God. So the real question is: Did God choose to become a man? Not, can he? The claim is that God became a man. It is amazing that so many rabbinical writings about Jesus refuse to discuss this very point and insist, instead, on discussing how a man could become God.

Other common objections also miss the real point.

One such objection is the fact that Jesus forgave sins which is something only God can do. Again this is true—only God can forgive sins. But if Jesus is the God-Man, God who became a man, the forgiving of sins would be part of the authority of this God-Man.

Another objection of this nature centers around the fact that Jesus performed his miracles in his own name. This objection, as voiced by one Jewish writer, runs as follows:

> The Hebrew prophets too, performed miracles; but they stressed that they did so as God's instruments. When Elijah revived the son of the widow, he did not say that he had wrought that miracle as Jesus did on a similar occasion.

First of all, it might be said that many times Jesus claimed that he was doing his miracles by the power and authority of the Spirit of God. It is true that the prophets did miracles and gave God the credit, but again, Messiah was not going to be just another man or just another prophet. Rabbinical theories taught that the Messiah, because he had the name of God himself, will be able to do things in his own name. That is why the Messiah kept playing such a prominent role in rabbinical theology. That is why the Jewish people throughout the centuries before modern liberalism crept into Judaism, continually looked forward to the coming of the Jewish Messiah. The Messiah would have such authority and such power that he would be able to accomplish great things in his own name. Jesus claimed to be that Messiah and so should in fact have been able to do those things in his own name. As the author admits, Jesus did accomplish those things in his own name. By doing so in his own name, he substantiates his messiahship rather than disproving it.

Poor Research

Other Jewish objections to Jesus show some very poor research with regard to what the New Testament is saying. One example reads like this: "Judaism . . . is committed to a good life and discourages asceticism. Jesus however claimed that his kingdom was not of this world: he pointed to poverty as the mark of piety."

The fact is that Jesus discouraged asceticism. He did encourage moderation in all things. The very purpose of the coming of Jesus was to provide enjoyment of life. Jesus said: "I have come that you might have life and that you might have it more abundantly " (John 10:10). He never at any time made poverty the mark of piety. He often talked against the false use of riches, but he never made wealth itself a sin or poverty a virtue. The message of Christ was not: Be good now so you can go to heaven later. His message was: Get right with God so you can enjoy the kind of life God wants you to enjoy.

Another example involving poor research of the New Testament is one that reads as follows: "Judaism exalts the family, integrated into a larger community. Jesus applauded celibacy and disparaged family ties as a barrier to religious dedication."

Actually, Jesus did not encourage celibacy. This type of life, Jesus said, was just for the very few; it was not a mark of higher spirituality. His main point was correct priorities. His teaching was this: Every person must put God first and his family second. This is hardly going contrary to Judaism.

Not only do some objections show poor research of the New Testament, they also show poor research of the Old Testament, as is clear in the following case:

> The Hebrew Bible emphasized unity of mankind and the prophets spoke as God's messengers to all nations and not primarily to his own people. Jesus, however, emphasized that he was sent only to the lost sheep of the house of Israel. He refused to heal the daughter of a Canaanite woman. Judaism does not discriminate against non-Jews.

One wonders if this writer ever read the Old Testament or even knows about his own Judaism. Judaism forbids intermarriage, and that is a form of discrimination against non-Jews. Furthermore, the prophets emphasized no such things as the writer claims. By far, the great majority of the Hebrew prophets did not give their messages to Gentiles but exclusively to the Jewish people. Over and over again, the prophets stressed the point that the Jews are God's people in a peculiar way and distinct from the Gentiles. There were messages that were for the Gentile nations, but these were invariably messages of judgment because of Gentile mistreatment of the Jewish people. One need only read the prophets through one time to see this.

The writer is also wrong about Jesus' dealings with the Canaanite woman. Jesus did not refuse to heal the daughter; in fact, he goes right ahead and does heal the daughter! The point that Jesus wanted to make to the Canaanite woman was that the Messiah's task was primarily to make himself known to the Jews, not the Gentiles. Gentiles would also be blessed, but never-

theless, Messiah's first priority was to the Jewish people.
The same is true with the Jewish prophets.

It would be futile to go on and on, for many of the
objections to the Messiahship of Jesus are based on
preconceived notions as to what the New Testament
claims rather than on what it actually states. The theological questions can best be answered after determining
the kind of God one believes in. Is God limited as to
what he can do or can he do any thing in accordance
with his power? Then it can be asked: Did God become
a man in Jesus or did he not? The Old Testament, not
modern Judaism, must be the standard by which it is
decided whether Jesus is the Messiah or not. This is
a question that no individual can honestly answer unless
he makes his own personal investigation. Rejection on
the basis of preconceived notions because of the way
one has been led to believe is dishonest to the person
himself.

The Majority and the Minority

A different kind of objection is raised over and over
again: If Jesus was the Messiah, why don't the rabbis
believe in him? Or it may be stated like this: If Jesus
is the Messiah, how come very few Jews believe this?
The implication here is that something cannot be true
for the Jew unless most rabbis or most Jewish people
accept it to be true. In other words, the implication is
that truth is determined by majority vote.

However, truth is not determined by majority vote.
If something is true, it is going to be true if everybody
believes it or if nobody believes it. Even if everybody
believes that the earth is flat and it is possible to fall

off the edge of the earth, it will still not make it true. Truth just cannot be determined that way. Truth is something that is absolute. It never changes. It is irrelevant how many people believe the truth. It is still true because of what it is in itself.

But some will say that if the Jewish religious leaders have rejected something, it certainly cannot be true religiously speaking, at least not for the Jews. If Jesus really was the Messiah, maybe not all Jews would have believed but certainly a great many should have, especially Jewish leaders. Well, as a matter of fact, a great many of the Jews did believe that Jesus was the Messiah, including Jewish leaders. No, it was not the majority. The majority rejected his messiahship. But a great many did accept his messiahship. Again, just because the majority did not accept Jesus as the Messiah, does not disqualify him from being the one.

As we look at our sacred history, we will discover over and over again that it was always the minority of Jews who obeyed the revelation of God. The prophets called the small group of believers the Remnant of Israel. It was always the remnant of Israel that accepted what God has to say through his prophets. The majority by and large has always rejected it, including the religious leaders of that day.

Let me give you an example that comes from the time of Elijah the prophet. As we look into the life of Elijah the prophet in the First Book of the Kings, chapter nineteen, we find Elijah very depressed because the people would not return to the God of Israel and worship him. Elijah's depression caused Elijah to run away to Mt. Sinai wishing he could die. He complains to God and says:

> I have been very jealous for Jehovah, the God of hosts; for
> the children of Israel have forsaken thy covenant, thrown down
> thine altars, and slain prophets with the sword: and I, even I
> only, am left; and they seek my life, to take it away. (vs. 10,14)

So completely was the nation of Israel given over to
idolatry in Elijah's day, that Elijah feels that he is all
alone. But God answers him and says: "Yet will I leave
me seven thousand in Israel, all the knees which have not
bowed unto Baal and every mouth which hath not kissed
him" (vs. 18).

The answer of God to Elijah is that there are seven
thousand others besides himself that have stayed true to
the God of Israel. Now notice, of the hundreds of
thousands of Jews living in the nation of Israel in Elijah's
day, only seven thousand believed the prophet Elijah.
Certainly here, the majority of the Jewish leaders were
wrong and again it was the remnant who believed.

When we come to the major prophets, we find the same
thing to be true. Even Isaiah, the prince of all the
prophets, said in his very first chapter: "Except Jehovah
of hosts had left unto us a very small remnant, we should
have been like unto Gomorrah" (vs. 9).

Isaiah, too, recognized that there is only a remnant,
a small minority of Jewish people which obeys the
prophets. The majority are in disobedience. Isaiah also
testifies that if it was not for this remnant, God would
have been so disgusted with Israel that he would have
destroyed us completely as he destroyed Sodom and

Gomorrah. The same thing could be said for the other prophets like Jeremiah and Ezekiel. All these prophets had to constantly go against the greater majority over and over again trying to maintain the truth of God.

Rabbi Saul, who was a Jewish believer from the first century, recognized that the very same thing was happening in his day. It was the minority of Jews who were accepting the Messiah Jesus. In one of his letters to a congregation in Rome, he recounts the story of Elijah and applies the story to his day. He says:

> Or know ye not what the scripture saith of Elijah? how he pleaded with God against Israel: Lord, they have killed thy prophets, they have digged down thine altars; and I am left alone, and they seek my life. But what saith the answer of God unto him? I have left for myself seven thousand men, who have not bowed the knee to Baal. Even so then at this present time also there is a remnant according to the election of grace (Rom. 11:2b-5).

Rabbi Saul explains that what was happening in his day and is happening today is what has always happened in Jewish history. The majority have always been disobedient to the revelation of the God of Israel. The minority, the remnant, have always believed. Rabbi Saul goes on to say that the Hebrew Christians are the believing Remnant of Israel today.

This type of truth, the truth of God, cannot be determined by the majority. So the answer is: So what if the majority of the rabbis and Jewish people do not accept Jesus as their Messiah. It does not change the fact that he is the Messiah.

The Logic of It All

But often the objection is raised that it is not logical, it is not Jewish to believe in Jesus. Well, that depends on the issue of who Jesus really is. Now suppose Jesus really is the Messiah. For the sake of argument, let the premise be allowed that he is the Messiah. Surely then the most natural, Jewish thing to do is to believe in him—that is logical enough. If Jesus is the Messiah, it is Jewish to believe in Jesus. And believing in Jesus if he is the Messiah makes a Jewish person not less Jewish but more Jewish. That actually makes him a completed Jew, because he has the relationship that the first Jew had, a relationship with God by faith.

Many objections raised are often fronts for a real objection that is not often voiced: the fear that if one who is Jewish accepts Jesus, he will cease to be a Jew. This is a real Jewish fear: He will cease to be a Jew and become a Gentile. Yet those Jews who do believe in Jesus firmly maintain that Jesus did not destroy their Jewishness. Therefore, in the next chapter we will discuss the question of Jewishness.

7.
Jewishness: What's It All About

One recurring theme in Jewish circles lately is a concern to define Jewishness. This issue has arisen because of political and religious conflicts in Israel. Neither the rabbinical authorities nor the political leaders of Israel have been able to come up with a definition that is agreeable to all.

Conflicting Definitions

The number of possible definitions range from the strictly religious to the strongly nationalistic. There is all the difference in the world as to whether one calls himself a Jewish American or an American Jew.

There are those who demand strictly a religious definition. These are inconsistent, however, in that they claim that Jews who profess to be atheists are still Jewish. It is ironic that those Jews who consider themselves anti-religious in Israel are still considered Jews by the ones who demand a strictly religious definition of Jewishness. Yet these would rule out a Christian Jew, in spite of the fact that the Hebrew Christian and the Orthodox Jew have far more in common religiously than the Orthodox Jew and the atheist Jew. For these reasons as well as others, defining Jewishness from a purely religious point of view does not satisfactorily explain who is a Jew. Judaism may be said to be the religion of many Jews, but it is no longer safe to say that it is the religion of most Jews. All Jews cannot be defined as such on the basis of Judaism simply because most Jews do not practice Judaism. And if the *practice* of Judaism was the distinguishing mark of Jewishness, many Hebrew Christians would certainly qualify; they are more faithful in the practice of Judaism than most Reform Jews.

The classical Zionist definition is that Jews are a people and a nation. Since most Zionist leaders have been atheists, religion, that is, Judaism, has been played down in the Zionist movement. They concluded from their view of history that Jews compose a national entity. They claimed that the answer to the Jewish problem was a national home for the Jews, and so the movement towards establishing a Jewish state began which culminated with the establishment of Israel in 1948.

But even the Zionists became inconsistent when they claimed that any Jew who believes in Jesus is no longer a Jew. How a person can lose his nationality by believing in Jesus never was explained. After all, Germans, Russians, and Italians who accept Jesus remain nationally Germans, Russians, and Italians. So it should be with the Jews. But logic has never been a virtue in the defining of Jewishness.

All definitions seem to fall short at some point. Tremendous confusion has resulted from every attempt to settle the issue. How much confusion there is became evident when the *Jerusalem Post* conducted a survey of fifteen hundred Jewish families with the question, Who or what is a Jew? The results were reported in the November 25, 1968, issue of the *Jerusalem Post:*

12% declared that a Jew was a person whose father or mother was a Jew or had a Jewish spouse.

23% said a Jew was one who considers himself a Jew.

19% held that according to religious law one who is born to a Jewish mother or converts to Judaism is a Jew.

13% said someone who observes Jewish religious practices.

13% said a Jew is one who lives in Israel or who identifies with the Jewish State.

11% answered that a Jew was one who was raised and educated as a Jew.

9% said they did not know.

In this public opinion poll conducted by the *Jerusalem Post,* six different definitions were offered. This certainly does show confusion in Jewish ranks when it comes to defining who is a Jew.

Nor are these the only definitions offered. One rabbi recently stated on television in New York that a Jew is simply anyone who is in favor of the ongoing and the continuation of the Jewish people. Under that definition a good number of Gentiles would qualify as well, for many Gentiles are very much in favor of the ongoing and continuation of the Jewish people! This rabbi went on to imply that God is totally unnecessary in Judaism—one could be an atheist and still be a follower of Judaism by reconstructing Judaism for himself, thus qualifying as a Jew. He did not explain how, if one Jew could reconstruct Judaism and rule God out and still be a Jew, another could not reconstruct Judaism and include Jesus and still be a Jew. This rabbi, with the inconsistency so prevalent today in defining Jewishness, ruled out Jews who believe in Jesus as Jews.

So while there is tremendous disagreement on the part of Jewish leaders as to who is a Jew, they generally tend to agree on one point: that Jews who believe in Jesus are no longer Jews. But this is really trying to define Jewishness by what it is not rather than by what it is. It is a fallacy to define something by what it is not, unless it is first defined as to what it is. In logic, one does not say A is not non-A without first stating that A is A. Until the Jewish leadership first defines what a Jew is, they are in no position to declare what a Jew is not.

The Reason for the Conflict

An answer to the question of why there is so much confusion as to the issue of who or what is a Jew might lie in the lack of an objective standard. Definitions tend to assume objective standards. One must first have an objective standard. Then the objective standard can be applied to an issue to see if the issue measures up correctly or not. At one time Judaism had an objective standard, and when it used that objective standard, there was never any question as to who or what is a Jew. That objective standard was the Jewish Scriptures. But during the last few centuries, Judaism departed more and more from the Scriptures with the end result that Judaism lost the objective standard it once had. And because it has gone away from the objective standard of the Scriptures, it has been unable to define itself, unable to say who is a Jew. Most Jews feel that they know they are Jews, but those very same Jews cannot say why they are Jews. As a result, they give many different answers.

Soon one ends up with agnosticism, which means one does not know. The fact that Jewish leaders give so many different answers show that they do not know. The reason they do not seem to know is because they do not have an objective standard to fall back on. The reason they have no objective standard is because they departed from the objective standard they once had: The Jewish Scriptures. The further any segment of Judaism departs the less sure, the less clear the definition. Finally, they must resort to defining a Jew by what he is not. They do not know what he is. To define Jewishness as not believing in Jesus is a cop-out.

Who Is a Jew?

By going back to the Jewish Scriptures, which are the source of Jewishness, we have an objective standard. Once this is done, the definition of Jewishness becomes easy. The biblical basis of defining Jewishness lies in the Abrahamic Covenant found in Genesis 12:1-3:

Now Jehovah said unto Abram, Get thee out of thy country, and from thy kindred, and from thy father's house, unto the land that I will show thee: and I will make of thee a great nation, and I will bless thee, and make thy name great; and be thou a blessing: and I will bless them that bless thee, and him that curseth thee will I curse: and in thee shall all the families of the earth be blessed.

In relation to Abraham, it is further described in two other passages:

For all the land which thou seest, to thee will I give it, and to thy seed for ever. And I will make thy seed as the dust of the earth: so that if a man can number the dust of the earth, then may thy seed also be numbered (Gen. 13:15-16).

And, behold, the word of Jehovah came unto him, saying, This man shall not be thine heir; but he that shall come forth out of thine own bowels shall be thine heir. And he brought him forth abroad, and said, Look now toward heaven, and number the stars, if thou be able to number them: and he said unto him, So shall thy seed be (Gen. 15:4-5).

Later the Abrahamic Covenant was confirmed through Isaac:

And Jehovah appeared unto him, and said, Go not down into Egypt; dwell in the land which I shall tell thee of: sojourn in this land, and I will be with thee, and will bless thee; for unto thee, and unto thy seed, I will give all these lands, and I will establish the oath which I sware unto Abraham thy father; and I will multiply thy seed as the stars of heaven, and will give unto thy seed all these lands; and in thy seed shall all the nations of the earth be blessed; because that Abraham obeyed my voice, and kept my charge, my commandments, my statutes, and my laws (Gen. 26:2-5).

After Isaac, the Abrahamic Covenant is reconfirmed through Jacob:

And, behold, Jehovah stood above it, and said, I am Jehovah, the God of Abraham thy father, and the God of Isaac: the land whereon thou liest, to thee will I give it, and to thy seed; and thy seed shall be as the dust of the earth, and thou shalt spread abroad to the west, and to the east, and to the north, and to the south: and in thee and in thy seed shall all the families of the earth be blessed (Gen. 28:13-14).

In the Abrahamic Covenant, a simple definition of Jewishness can be found in the repeated statements that a nation will come through the line of Abraham, Isaac, and Jacob. Jewishness would then be defined as nationality. But unlike the view of many Zionists, this nationality is not confined to the State of Israel alone; it includes all the Jewish people no matter where they are. It is a nationality based on descendancy, not on history nor on Zionism.

Biblically speaking, the Jewish people are a nation. Today we are a scattered nation, but we are, nevertheless, a nation because we are descendants of Abraham, Isaac, and Jacob. By this definition, no matter what the individual Jewish person may believe or disbelieve, he remains a Jew. The implication here is that no matter what a Jew does, he can never become a non-Jew. A Negro who is a Christian remains a Negro. A Negro who becomes a Moslem remains a Negro. A Negro who becomes a Buddhist remains a Negro. A Chinese man who becomes a Christian remains Chinese. A Chinese man who becomes a Buddhist also remains Chinese. The same is true of the Jewish person. He is a Jew because he is a descendant of Abraham, Isaac, and Jacob. Whether Orthodox, Reform, atheist, or Communist, he remains a Jew. If a Jew chooses to believe that Jesus is his Messiah, he remains a Jew. Nothing, absolutely nothing, can change the fact that he is a descendant of Abraham, Isaac, and Jacob.

Who Is a Gentile?

If this is the definition of Jewishness, what then is a Gentile? If the Scriptures are again used as the objective standard, a Gentile is simply anyone who is not a descendant of Abraham, Isaac, and Jacob. A Gentile is anyone not born a Jew. The implication again is that no matter what a Gentile does, he can never become a non-Gentile.

Who Is a Christian?

If the above definition is true, it should become apparent that "Gentile" and "Christian" are not synonymous terms. Most Gentiles in the West call themselves Christians, but this does not make it true. It is not enough to simply claim to be a Christian. Because many non-Christians call themselves Christians, *who is a Christian* has become just as much a confused issue in many circles as *who is a Jew* is in other circles.

This confusion is, again, due to a departure from an objective standard. To determine who is a Christian, one must go to the New Testament, the source of what Christianity is all about.

The New Testament divides the world into three groups of people: Jews, Gentiles, and Christians (1 Cor. 10:32). Everyone is either born a Jew or a Gentile, but no one is ever born a Christian. A Christian is a person, either a Jew or a Gentile, who has made a personal decision to become a Christian, a follower of Christ (Messiah). A Christian is not one who merely holds church membership or is baptized. These acts may follow the decision a person makes to become a Christian, but they cannot be the cause of becoming a Christian.

The New Testament teaches that a Christian is a Jew or a Gentile who has come to realize that man is born in a state of sin and for this reason he is separated from God. As a result, to come to know God in a personal way, the inquirer must recognize that a penalty for sin must first be paid. However, being a sinner, an individual, whether a Jew or a Gentile, cannot by himself pay the price or penalty for sin. For this purpose the Messiah, whom many Jews and Gentiles know to be Jesus, came. At Messiah's death, he became the substitute for sin and so paid the penalty for sin.

The Scriptures teach, both in the Old and New Testaments, that without the shedding of blood there is no forgiveness of sin:

> For the life of the flesh is in the blood; and I have given it to you upon the altar to make atonement for your souls: for it is the blood that maketh atonement by reason of the life (Old Testament—Lev. 17:11).

> And according to the law, I may almost say, all things are cleansed with blood, and apart from shedding of blood there is no remission (New Testament—Heb. 9:22).

The basic content of faith, that is, what one must believe, is found in 1 Corinthians 15:1-4:

> Now I make known unto you, brethren, the gospel which I preached unto you, which also ye received, wherein also ye stand, by which also ye are saved, if ye hold fast the word which I preached unto you, except ye believed in vain. For I delivered unto you first of all that which also I received: that Christ died for our sins according to the scriptures; and that he was buried; and that he hath been raised on the third day according to the scriptures.

The content of faith is the gospel, involving the substitutionary death, burial, and resurrection of Christ. The act that determines whether or not a person is a Christian is his willingness to place his faith, or belief, in Jesus as the substitute for sin. What he must do is spelled out in John 1:12: "But as many as received him, to them gave he the right to become children of God, even to them that believe on his name."

A person who at some point in his life personally receives Christ as the one who made atonement for his sin experiences what it is to become a Christian. Hence, if anyone says that he was born a Christian, it is an obvious sign, according to the New Testament, that he is not in fact a Christian, since no one is born a Christian. Becoming a Christian is an experience by which one comes to know God through Jesus Christ, and the sin which has separated the individual from God is thus removed. Hence, Christians are made, not born.

In summary, then, the New Testament teaches that every one is born either a Jew or a Gentile. Christians are those who personally receive Jesus as the substitute sacrifice for their sins. This could very well mean that most people who call themselves Christians really are not. That is why, due to the confusion of so many who say they are and are not, those who are true Christians, in the New Testament sense of the term, have begun to employ the term *believer*. This is in order to better distinguish those who are truly Christians as over against those who merely claim to be.

What Is a Hebrew Christian?

So what is a Hebrew Christian? To most Jewish minds, the term "Hebrew Christian" is a contradiction in terms. They think that one can be either Jewish or Christian but to be both at the same time is an impossibility. What then is a Hebrew Christian? If a Jew is a descendant of Abraham, Isaac, and Jacob, and a Christian is one who has personally on his own volition accepted

Jesus as his Messiah, then a Hebrew Christian is a Jew who believes that Jesus Christ is his Messiah. In terms of faith, Hebrew Christians align themselves with other believers in Christ whether they be Jews or Gentiles. Nationally they identify themselves with the Jewish people.

A Hebrew Christian, then, must acknowledge himself to be both a Jew and a Christian. If a Jewish person accepts baptism solely on the basis of attempting to lose his identity as a Jew, he is by no means to be considered a Hebrew Christian. A Hebrew Christian is proud of his Jewish heritage and of his faith in his Messiah.

Rabbi Saul, better known as the apostle Paul, has often been accused of making faith in Christ a Gentile religion. Many rabbis have written to say that while Jesus himself was okay, and even that he was very Jewish, Paul spoiled it all by turning the messianic movement of Jesus into a Gentile religion. Paul declared in his writings, however, that God was the one who commanded him to preach about the Messiah to the Gentiles. The best evidence, however, that he was strongly nationalistic and loyal to the Jewish people is Paul's own writings. Let us examine excerpts from three separate writings of the apostle Paul:

I say then, Did God cast off his people? God forbid. For I also am an Israelite, of the seed of Abraham, of the tribe of Benjamin (Rom. 11:1).

Are they Hebrews? so am I. Are they Israelites? so am I. Are they the seed of Abraham? so am I (2 Cor. 11:22).

I yet more: circumcised the eighth day, of the stock of Israel, of the tribe of Benjamin, a Hebrew of Hebrews; as touching the law, a Pharisee, as touching zeal, persecuting the church;

as touching the righteousness which is in the law, found
blameless. Howbeit what things were gain to me, these have
I counted loss for Christ. Yea verily, and I count all things
to be loss for the excellency of the knowledge of Christ Jesus
my Lord: for whom I suffered the loss of all things, and do
count them but refuse, that I may gain Christ (Phil. 3:4-8).

It would be hard indeed from these statements to
force upon Paul blame for making the Christian faith
a Gentile religion.

In the next chapter we will share some of the experiences of Jews who believe in Jesus today. It will become
evident that their belief in Jesus has made them more
Jewish, not less.

8.
What Jesus Has Done for Jewish Lives

According to the Old Testament, the purpose of the first coming of the Messiah was for him to die for the sins of the Jewish people. The New Testament declares that indeed this is what Jesus did do. The Old Testament further declared in Isaiah 53 that those who will accept the substitutionary death and resurrection of the Messiah will receive justification, spiritual healing, and be reconciled with God. If Jesus is the Messiah, then the lives of those Jews who accepted Jesus and his messiahship, should undergo a change for the better. According to the Old Testament, this should be the result for those who accept the atonement of the Messiah's blood on their behalf.

This is exactly what has been happening with Jewish people throughout the centuries; it is also happening today on a large scale. It is happening among the old, the young, and the middle-aged; among the Orthodox, the Conservatives, the Reform, and among the nonaffiliated; the atheists, the agnostics, and among the New Left. Several have written down an account of their experiences—we will let them tell their own stories.

The Adult World
Asher Levi—Ex-Rabbi
I was a Sephardic Jewish Rabbi for a period of thirty-

five years. Born in Sarajevo-Bosnia, in Yugoslavia, I was reared in a most Orthodox Jewish home. I learned to recite conventional prayers and to wear phylacteries, which are enjoined upon every devout Jew. At the age of fifteen, I entered the Theological School for Rabbis, where I was duly trained in the Old Testament and Talmudic Commentaries. I was ordained at the age of twenty-one and had my first pulpit in Ploesti, Romania. Successively I served in Antwerp, Belgium; London, England; and in Los Angeles, California, which was my last synagogue here in the United States.

Outwardly I was happy and successful in my work—I got on pretty well—but inwardly I was restless and dissatisfied, for I suffered much from an inadequacy about life in general. So it happened when I was in Miami Beach, Florida, six years ago, I came in contact with a Jew who I did not know was a believer in Christ and asked him to advise me about my situation. His reply was: "Read Isaiah chapter 53." I read this famous chapter concerning Jesus of Nazareth which said "he was wounded for our transgressions, he was bruised for our iniquities." Yet, I felt constrained to search the Hebrew Scriptures, and I found the words of Isaiah, saying:

For unto us a child is born, unto us a son is given: and the government shall be upon his shoulder: and his name shall be called Wonderful, Counsellor, the Mighty God, The Everlasting Father, The Prince of Peace. Of the increase of his government and peace there shall be no end, upon the throne of David, and upon his kingdom, to order it, and to establish it with judgment and with justice from henceforth even for ever (Isa. 9:6-7).

In addition I read:

Hear ye now, O house of David . . . the Lord himself shall give you a sign; Behold, a virgin shall conceive, and bear a son, and shall call his name Immanuel (Isa. 7:13-14).

"Immanuel" means "God with us."

This gave me the assurance that Jesus indeed is the Messiah in whom has been fulfilled all the prophets' predictions. Meanwhile, I got a clear picture of the Messiah when I had the opportunity to hold in my hands a little book which I found to be the New Testament—a book about which I knew almost nothing. I began to read it the same way I would read any other book. I began at the beginning and read the words: "The book of the generation of Jesus Christ, the son of David, the son of Abraham. . . ." I found to my surprise that I was reading a Jewish book about a Jew. Reading gradually, I came to the conclusion that Jesus was a Jew of the seed of Abraham and David; that Jesus was born of a Jewish virgin, in a Jewish town, Bethlehem, into a Jewish tribe, the tribe of Judah. I realized that Jesus knew the Law and the Prophets, so I followed him around reading and learning his beautiful sayings and teachings as he traveled, taught, and healed in the hills and valleys of the Holy Land, which became as spiritual food to me. His promise of forgiveness and eternal life to those who believe in him drew me until one day I put my trust in him, and I accepted him as my Messiah and my personal Savior from my sins.

I have to assert that my heart does not condemn me for my new faith, for I feel I still am a Jew and never will cease to be a Jew. I did not abandon our heritage of Abraham, Isaac, and Jacob. Like Paul, I am able to say even after accepting the Christ: "Are they Hebrews? So am I. Are they Israelites? So am I. Are they the offspring of Abraham? So am I."

Mary Linderman—Executive Secretary

Until June, 1967, I knew God only as someone who lived way up in heaven. Then an unexpected surgery and a broken engagement left me physically and emotionally drained. My life seemed shattered. Everything I did to regain the happiness I had formerly known plunged me into deeper despair.

When all else had failed, I found myself praying to God. For the first time in my life I earnestly searched for him. God answered my prayers, but not in the way I had expected.

God reached down and touched me with the fullness of his presence through his Son, the Messiah. His love—so pure and real—poured through me to overflowing. Life took on a new meaning and purpose. Every day began to be filled with promise and hope.

I found that I did not have to give up my Jewish heritage in order to accept Christ. He just added a new dimension of peace and understanding to my life.

Bob Charness—Businessman

Is it possible for an agnostic to find God? I did.

Although I was born and raised in a Jewish home, I had no interest in God or his scriptures. My Jewish heritage meant so little to me that I seldom really participated in the holidays.

Then one day I discovered the Messiah's love for me.

My life changed, and for the first time God became a living reality. I felt more Jewish than I had ever felt in my life.

My mother and sister began to carefully observe the change that took place in my home. A new love radiated both my wife's and my spiritual experience. As my mother and sister watched, they too responded to Christ's love.

Our Jewishness has been made complete in Christ.

Ruby Charness—Homemaker

God has been wonderful to me. I marvel at the way he has supplied my every need day by day.

There was a time when I was frightened and did not want to accept the responsibility for my home, my children, or even my own life. Now God has given me the confidence and wisdom to face life's problems with a peace that only Christ can give.

I have found that by trusting the Messiah I am able to do many things I had thought were impossible. Even though I loved to play the guitar and sing, my fear of audiences kept me from performing. Now I have sung and played for as many as five thousand people.

But more important is the joy of knowing that whatever may happen, God works out everything to the good for those who love and follow him.

Irv Rifkin—Minister

Perhaps some would call me "a typical Jewish boy." I was raised in a fairly religious home, rebelled at having to attend cheder, and **Bar Mitzvah** at thirteen. After that my religious education ceased.

Occasionally I attended the synagogue for the holidays, but I lacked spiritual fulfillment. My search for spiritual reality began when my mother died.

Her death made me desire to know more about eternal life. No one seemed to have definite answers, not even the rabbis.

It wasn't until nearly six years later that I began looking for the answers in the Old and New Testaments. As I read the Scriptures, I discovered that God had sent Christ as my Messiah in order to give me eternal life. Since accepting him I have found spiritual reality, and the Scriptures have become alive to me.

Dr. Vera Schlamm—Pediatrician

Why me? Why should I have survived two of Hitler's concentration camps when six million of my people had perished?

My determination to find what God wanted of me led to an investigation of the Torah. There I discovered that it was impossible to keep all the laws, yet that seemed to be what God required.

I continued reading until I reached the prophets. I was surprised to read Isaiah's declaration that a child would be born who would be called, "The mighty God, The Everlasting Father, The Prince of Peace." Isaiah 53 held even greater surprise for me. It spoke in terms that could only be applied to Christ. But I did not want to accept this.

Then one morning the love of the Messiah touched my heart. Without understanding any theology, I believed and turned my heart over to Christ. Since that time he has given me peace in all circumstances of life.

Sid Becker—Retired Executive

The greatest event of my life is centered in the day I came to accept the Messiah as my Savior.

I was born and raised on the lower eastside of New York City. While growing up, our family observed all the Jewish holidays.

In 1938 my wife and I moved to the West Coast. I believe God led us there to prepare us for the tragic death of our son only six years later in World War II.

It was through his loss that we began to search for a closer relationship to God. I attended a church several times with my wife and became interested in the Scriptures. I began to study both the Old and New Testaments. I checked and rechecked what I read and became convinced that Jesus was really the Messiah.

In Christ I have found peace of mind and heart. He has given me more tolerance, more patience, and a love for my fellowman.

Rose Becker—Homemaker

The way that ultimately led me to God was marked by illness and sorrow.

When World War II broke out, my oldest son enlisted. I did not see him again for two years. When I became seriously ill, he obtained a leave to visit me, and that was the last time I ever saw him. Four months later he was killed in action.

In my sorrow I turned to God for consolation and hope. One day I visited a large temple in Los Angeles. As the rabbi read from the book of Isaiah my eyes fell on the words, "Behold, a young woman shall conceive and bear a son, and his name shall be called Immanuel."

I thought to myself, "This speaks of Jesus." When I returned home I began to search the Scriptures. Passage after passage confirmed my conclusion.

A short time later I experienced the love of Christ in my life. Since that time I have known a peace and joy I never thought possible.

Leon Brooks—Meat Cutter

I was raised in a Jewish home and had always considered myself a good person. Then came the day I first faced the stark reality that I was estranged from God.

Was it possible for a modern, twentieth-century man to find peace with himself and God?

I turned to a psychiatrist for an answer. He suggested that I was not responsible for my actions. He proposed that I was the net result of the genealogical traits I had inherited from my ancestors.

My parents and friends also afforded me little comfort. Now I know that only God could take away my burden and guilt.

Eventually I turned to the Scriptures. There I discovered every man is separated from God. In the Old Testament law, God required a blood sacrifice for sins. Then the Messiah came to give himself as a sacrifice for us.

I accepted Christ's sacrifice for me, and since that time my life has been filled with peace and joy.

Rita Crawshaw—Homemaker

The name of Jesus was not new to me. My father was a well-known cantor in Russia, and as a girl I can remember that we had to pray for the czar in the name of Esues Xhristoes.

I married a fine, young English Jew and God blessed us with four children. We lived in China until my husband and I were wounded by Chinese bandits. I was in the hospital a long time before I learned that my husband had passed away.

Although I was able to move to America and raise my children, life seemed incomplete. I began to search—for what I did not know. I continued to search for nearly five years until I discovered that life was incomplete without the Messiah.

I accepted Christ and experienced a fullness of life for which I had been longing. He brought me into the presence of God and filled my life with joy and peace.

Paul Herme—Businessman

My wife's decision to accept Christ filled me with apprehension.

I could not help but notice the changes that began to occur in my wife. She was happy, joyful, and filled with a radiance I had never seen before.

I accepted Christ and the reality of God's love touched my life too.

Leonore Herme—Homemaker

Christ has filled my life with a peace and love I never knew existed. Since coming to him, I have experienced a sense of purpose and direction which has changed my life. Each day he gives me joy and strength to touch other people's lives with his love.

Delores Herme—Secretary

My search for happiness and peace of mind led me to Israel, Switzerland, England, and back to the United States. Upon returning home, I despaired at having failed so miserably to achieve my goal.

Then one day I discovered that Christ could put it all together in my life. Now I face each day with peace and happiness.

Lillian Muslin—Homemaker

Sometimes I wondered if there even was a God or if he just existed in people's imagination.

I had been seeking him for a long time, but a vacuum continued to remain in my heart. God seemed faraway, and as hard as I tried I could not feel anything personal about him.

Then one day our son came home singing about Jesus. We went to investigate the Jewish club where he had been learning the songs. There we met a group of Jews who believed Jesus was the Messiah.

We began to study the Bible, and the Old Testament began to take on meaning as we learned about Israel and the promised Messiah. The teachings of the Bible became so clear and real that I began to feel the presence of God.

I accepted Jesus as my Messiah, and he came into my life. The vacuum I once experienced was filled by the Messiah's presence.

Morris Muslin—Retired Postal Employee

You can imagine my surprise when our nine-year-old

son returned from a Jewish children's club singing about Jesus.

When questioned about his actions, he assured me that he had been at a Jewish place and a Jewish lady was in charge. Naturally, I asked the lady who had invited my son to what kind of place she had taken him. She said it was a Jewish group that believed Jesus was the Messiah of Israel.

My wife and I decided to further investigate the matter, and it was here that we first learned about the prophecies of Christ.

All my life I had searched for something but did not know what. Through this Jewish group I learned that God sent the Messiah to give us a more abundant life.

I invited Christ into my heart, and since that time I have experienced a life abundantly full and complete.

Dr. L. Irwin Weissman—Physician
Christ's love upholds and sustains my wife and me throughout each day. We are able to walk with confidence and happiness knowing that he is with us wherever we may go.

Leah Cowdroy—Homemaker
I thank God that he has led each member of my family to his Son, the Messiah. Our entire family has been blessed by the joy of knowing that he will be with us throughout every circumstance of life.

Richard Hoffman—Student
My Jewish heritage meant more than ever to me after I came to know Christ.

He has also taught me how to accept myself, and he gives me power to overcome the problems of life.

Dr. Emil Gruen—Minister

Christ has given me the satisfaction of sharing the love and peace I found in him with my own people. Throughout my life, he has kept every promise he made in the Scriptures.

Mitchell Seidman—Aeronautical Engineer

My training and experience as an engineer have taught me to search for facts, to analyze them, and to find answers.

Sometimes, even in engineering and science, we make basic assumptions which cannot be proven. Why then are they accepted? The answer is that they work when put to a test whereas other assumptions fail.

I have personally investigated and tested God's promises in the Scriptures to see if they work. The Old Testament promises that anyone who searches for God can find him, if they search for him with all their heart.

Testing this promise, I have found that God does reveal himself to me through his Son, the Messiah. God is a living reality in my life, and as he has promised, I found peace and joy through the love of Christ.

How can a Jew believe in Christ? I have accepted him because what the Scriptures promised fits perfectly together with the facts of history and my personal experience has verified the promise of God's Messiah.

Naomi Seidman—Homemaker

I have often wondered why no one told me about

this other Jesus—the one who loved me.

I had heard about the one some people accused me of killing, and I had heard about the Jesus whose cross hung about necks of German soldiers as they put my people to death in the gas chambers. But, until I was a teenager, no one told me about the Jesus who loved me.

One night while at a summer camp, his love reached down and touched my heart, and I accepted him as my Messiah. Shortly afterward I discovered other members of my family had made similar decisions to accept Christ.

It's been eighteen years since the Messiah came into my life, and I can say that knowing him has made my life complete. God has abundantly blessed our family and home as we continue to follow him.

Jackie Pappas—Homemaker

My Jewish heritage was made complete and forever established in Christ. He has filled my life with an inspiration and a love that is difficult to explain.

Through Christ, I have found truth and meaning to life.

Sally Paris—Retired Businesswoman

Everyone needs a place of refuge. I found this shelter in the promised Messiah. He brought peace, hope, and purpose into my life. Now I look forward to that time when I shall see him face to face.

Maurice Benson—Businessman

I am proud of my Jewish heritage, and I have found

the answers to three of life's greatest questions in Christ. He showed me who I am, what God expects of me, and where I am going after death.

Samuel W. Brod—Businessman

I was raised in an Orthodox Jewish home, so for a year I fought the acceptance of Christ. Then one day his love touched me. Since that time I have learned, above all else, that I can depend upon him.

Leo Borden—Businessman

I had a very personal encounter with Christ. He stepped out of the pages of the Bible and into my life in such a manner that I was confronted with his reality.

This experience happened as I stood in a European church and prayed; "Dear Jesus, I am not of your faith, but I am very lost. I need your help. Can you help me?" At that moment I experienced an encounter with Christ not unlike that of Rabbi Saul in Tarsus nearly two thousand years ago.

But I could not accept Christ. I was a Jew, my parents were Jewish, and my grandparents were Orthodox. For over two years I avoided his call to me. Finally, I came to the place where I accepted him.

Christ stepped into my life, and today I am a much happier person than I ever was before I met him.

Fay Cohen—Secretary

I came from a very Orthodox background, so I could not understand how my daughter could accept Christ as the Messiah.

For nearly ten years, I rejected my daughter for her

decision. I wouldn't open the door when she came to see me. I hung up the phone when I heard her voice, and I immediately destroyed her letters.

During all this time, God was working in my life. Without knowing it, my attitude began to mellow. Eventually I agreed to attend a meeting. I was impressed by the warmth of the Hebrew Christians I met and began to study the Scriptures with them.

Then one day, God showed me that he hears and answers prayer when Christ touched my life. From that day to this, I was never more happy. The Messiah keeps the light in my eyes and the smile on my face.

Dan Delman—Real Estate Broker

In 1957 I began to read the Bible to see if it said what I had been told by a stranger.

As I read the New Testament, I was surprised to find that all the first followers of Jesus were Jewish. I also learned that he came to this earth as a sacrifice for man's sin. I continued reading.

While reading one day, I began to feel the presence of God. I stopped and prayed: "Almighty God, these things in this book seem to be true to me, and I want to believe if it is from you. I want to accept Jesus as my Messiah."

I didn't hear any voices, but God touched my life and I definitely knew it was there, that Jesus was my Messiah.

Since that time, I have continually felt the perfect peace that God promises to give to those who love him and follow his Son, the Messiah.

Shirley Delman—Homemaker

Toward the end of World War II, my husband was sent to Germany. In my distress I wanted to pray, but I didn't know how to approach God.

I had heard some strange stories about Jesus—how he healed the sick, raised the dead, and performed many other miracles. More than ever, what I needed was a miracle worker.

I began to pray to Jesus because I felt it would do no harm, and it might even work. My husband returned safely, but I forgot my promise to tell everyone what Jesus had done for me.

The next twelve years I read more about Jesus from time to time. Then God began to work in our lives. My husband began to read the Bible, and I began to listen to a religious radio broadcast. A short time later we both accepted Christ as our Messiah.

I can't fully express the peace and joy I have found since accepting him. He has been true to every one of his promises.

Barbara Benedict—Executive Secretary

One of the greatest things I have found in Christ is acceptance. He accepted me with all of my imperfections because he had created me and could perfect his own creation.

Truly Christ has touched my life with kindness and an everlasting love.

Alan Rosenberg—Minister

Initially my only motive for reading the New Testament was to find out what it contained, for I had been raised in a Jewish home and I took my Judaism seriously.

As I read, it became apparent that Christ was really my Messiah. I accepted him, and my life with him has been one of joy and peace. I have never felt even the slightest sense of regret that I accepted Christ as my Messiah.

Ann Applebaum—Homemaker

Through Christ I discovered that it was possible to establish a very close personal contact with God.

The Messiah has touched my life with peace, love, and assurance of eternal life.

Melicent Hunt—Homemaker

I could not accept the Bible because God required a sacrifice for sins. Yet, it was impossible to fulfill this requirement. Then I discovered that Christ came to give himself as a sacrifice for me.

I accepted him, and since that time I have marveled at his faithfulness and goodness.

Lee Amber—Actor

In spite of difficult moments, I have never regretted accepting Christ as my Messiah. Through him, the peace of God has become more and more real each day and I rejoice in his provision for every need.

For the first time in my life, I am happy to be Jewish, in fact, I feel more Jewish than ever before. I am secure in the knowledge that I have found eternal salvation through the Lord Jesus, my Messiah.

Henrietta Thompson—Secretary

Christ not only gave me the peace for which I had
been searching, he gave me a promise to stand upon:
"Believe on the Lord Jesus Christ, and thou shalt be
saved, and thy house."

After nearly ten years, my mother was also touched
by the love of Christ. Since that time, other members
of our family have come to him. Surely he keeps his
promises. He never fails.

Anne Seidman—Homemaker

In 1940 I was suddenly arrested on life's highway
and brought face to face with the question of God and
his Christ. Until then, I had never heard that God cared
and was personally interested in every individual and
expected, yea, demanded more than mere acknowl-
edgment of his existence.

For the first time in my life I found myself calling
upon God. But I was shocked at his answer. It was Jesus.
How could Jesus be the answer when I was calling upon
the name of God?

Then God touched my heart and I realized that Jesus
was truth, he was peace, and he came offering me the
peace I longed for. A Holy God's gift of love to me.
For the veil had dropped from before my eyes, and
I beheld the glory of the only begotten Son of God,
Jesus the Messiah of Israel.

Now I arise each morning with a melody upon my
lips and a psalm in my heart.

Louis Seidman—Businessman

I was brought up in an Orthodox Jewish home and

studied in Hebrew school to a high school equivalent. I was taught to believe the Tenach was the Word of God and went with my parents to the synagogue regularly.

My studies, the synagogue services, and the holidays emphasized that God was holy, righteous, pure and sinless—and I was not.

One day a man came into my place of business and told me Jesus was the Messiah. He showed me Isaiah 53 and Proverbs 30:4. I went home and compared these verses to those in my Hebrew Bible. I could see that these verses did speak of the Messiah, and it was readily apparent to me that they described Jesus.

I accepted Christ as my Messiah, and I raised my children to be proud of their Jewish heritage and to believe in Jesus our Messiah.

Linda Cohen—Homemaker

My parents found it difficult to understand how I could accept Christ. They had sent me to religious school from the time I was four until I was fourteen.

Although I loved my mother very much and did not want to hurt her, I felt that I could not deny my belief that Christ had come as my Messiah.

The conflict of hurting my parents on one hand and rejecting Christ on the other deeply troubled me. Then one day it came to me that if God loved me so much that he gave his Son to die for my sins, he would love me enough to help me with my parents.

So I went ahead and accepted Jesus as my Messiah, and I have not regretted my decision to follow him. He has shown me his love by taking care of me day by day.

Richard Cohen—Minister

I did not have time for God and did not give him much thought.

When my wife and I went to a rabbi for premarital counselling, he asked me my beliefs. When we were through talking, he said I was so far from God that God would never find me. That was okay by me, because I didn't want God anyway.

Several months after we were married, my wife met a lady who told her about Christ. When I learned of the discussion, I became very angry. The lady then brought a Hebrew-Christian friend to discuss the matter with me. The only thing they accomplished was to make me angry.

They invited me to some meetings and I decided to go in order to prove them wrong. After nearly three months of studying, arguing, and discussing the matter, Christ became real to me. He came into my life, and I learned to love God through him.

David Hart—Men's Hairdresser

When my mother and aunt accepted Christ as their Messiah, I was very confused. I had been brought up as a Jew, and I didn't want to accept a Gentile god as I believed Jesus to be.

My mother and aunt were widowed, and I was relieved to see that they seemed to have found contentment and happiness after being so sad and lonely. I concluded that maybe this was for older and sad people, but not for a young, healthy Jew like me. I had no intention of ever being anything but a Jew.

One night I agreed to attend a meeting where I experienced the love of Christ in my life. I accepted him as my Messiah, and now I feel more Jewish than ever. I am also prouder of my heritage, and my life has been filled with God's blessing as I followed the Messiah.

The Young World

Shelley Korotkin

I was brought up in an upper middle-class Jewish home, the second of three girls. We had most everything we wanted or needed—a big house, nice clothes, devoted friends, cars, all of the things that make a good, middle-class Jewish home.

Growing up meant attending elementary school and Hebrew school, visiting friends, taking piano lessons, doing art, being a little bewildered and a little loud.

My dreams were to become a famous artist, get married, have children, and live happily ever after. I received a scholarship to the Academy of Fine Arts in my hometown of Philadelphia. A scholarship for a first-year student is really unusual, and I considered myself on the way to fulfilling a dream.

It was all very nice until the age of seventeen. At this time my life-style stopped supplying the mental, physical, and emotional needs that were growing in me. Life was no longer satisfying. My day-by-day routine was turning into day-by-day boredom. I was going through each day looking for something novel and stimulating to fill my life. I began to live from experience to experience.

My new outlook on life was to experience everything

but always be in control. I wanted to be the experienced but cool person who could cope with anything. That was easy enough to think and the game was easy to play, or so I thought.

My thought patterns were becoming more serious, less frivolous, as I was getting older. I was asking myself and my friends what was the purpose for living: What do I want to do in life? These questions would come and go according to my moods. My friends, however, didn't take my questions, moods, or me very seriously; but then I didn't take myself very seriously either most of the time.

During the past two years, I had watched my sister Lana go through an unusual change. She was two and one-half years older than I and had lived a similar life. The cause of her change was due to reading the Bible. I didn't like it even though she seemed happy. Instead of her former frustration, Lana had a peace about her which made me jealous and angry. Lana explained her change by saying that she had discovered Jesus, the Messiah. It seemed stupid to me. She had a good Jewish education and should have known better than to believe Gentile superstitions. I thought she had really flipped. I wanted no part of her new trip.

I believed in God all my life (at least a little bit). I had gone to Sunday School, Hebrew school, and was Bas Mitzvahed at thirteen. So far as I and the rest of my family were concerned, Jesus was just a man, and maybe he never existed at all.

Lana left the house and moved to New York City to be with other Jews who believed in Jesus. I was free of her and her piercing words, but not for long. Soon my mother and younger sister, Terry, were also reading the New Testament and talking about Jesus. My mother attended temple every sabbath and was soprano soloist for the choir. She should have known Judaism better than to believe in Jesus. It all seemed horrible. I was surrounded by Bibles and God-talk.

Whatever was in that Book was so alive that it was changing the lives of my family. I wanted to fight it, but my curiosity got the better of me.

I opened that Book and read through its pages about this so-called Son of God called Jesus. The name "Jesus" repulsed me, because my heart had been hardened to it for so long. However, if he was the Son of God and I could actually have a personal relationship with God, I wanted to know. So I prayed to God, and I prayed to Jesus and asked either of them to show me the truth. I was uncertain of what might happen, if anything.

God began to answer my prayer. Through his love, he came into my life. I started seeing life with new eyes. I experienced a spiritual birth. Life started to become a new and unimaginable adventure. the emptiness that was in me for so long was gone and was replaced with something very special that made me start becoming the person I really wanted to be. Life became full of purpose—love. And a sense of worth came to me.

I've been a believer for three years now, and not once has that emptiness ever returned. I've gone through hassles and lost some "friends" who felt threatened by my new beliefs.

I don't feel I have solved all the problems of my life, but I have a direction, ideals, and goals that I didn't have before. Jesus gave this to me. Through him I have become a real *mentsh* (authentic person).

Baruch Goldstein

My name is Baruch Goldstein. Baruch is the Hebrew name given to me at birth. I was born in New York City and was raised in the Bronx, a section you might call a ghetto—a Jewish ghetto. I went to Hebrew school for four years, until the time that I was Bar Mitzvahed.

Along with my Hebrew name, I was given the English name of Bruce; and for most of my life, I have been known as Bruce. But now, since I have come to know Jesus, who has made me more Jewish than ever before, I've decided to be called Baruch. It seems appropriate.

I grew up in a fast, changing world. There were a lot of things in the world which I did not understand and that I know were wrong. But what was right for the world I didn't know either, so I started searching.

At sixteen I got involved with drugs. In New York City this is easy to do. I graduated by the skin of my teeth and went on to college, only because there was nothing else to do. I didn't last there very long. I flunked out after one semester!

I was worried. The draft was breathing down my neck. I figured the smartest thing to do was to go into the Army, so I volunteered for the draft. I went the way of all good soldiers and found myself in Vietnam. I was in the infantry—the First Air Cavalry, a really gung-ho fighting unit. I was worried that I might get myself killed. For the first time in a long time I thought of God. I even found myself praying at times. I was asking God to help me, not for my sake particularly, but for my family. Because I knew how much it would grieve my parents if something happened to me.

I was in Vietnam only six weeks before I was wounded. We were assaulting a village. I wasn't beside my buddy where I was supposed to be, and I kept thinking that I should get up beside him. But when the rocket came in that wounded me, it landed right beside my buddy, killing him instantly.

It humbles me to know that God wants me alive for some reason and has called me for something, because it's a miracle that I'm alive and able to tell this story.

After I was wounded, I spent about seven months in hospitals and was discharged from the service.

As soon as I got out of Vietnam, I became involved again in drugs. Since I didn't have to worry about an income, because I received government disability checks, I took an extended vacation. I had to catch up on what was going on in life. My parents assumed the attitude, "Let the kid take off for a couple of months and then he'll settle down." The years went by and I didn't settle down. Life was still unexplainable, and I wanted to find meaning for it.

I started getting freaky—my hair got long, I grew a beard, and I acted outrageously. Eventually, I went the way of every good hippie and found myself in California, searching for I-don't-know-what.

I was different from most hippies, because I had an income. As a result, I always had a lot of friends around me. I sometimes wonder if it was because I had money or if they really were my friends. But being a good-natured person, this didn't really bother me. If I had something to share, I was willing to help.

I went to Sausalito (California) and wanted to build

a houseboat on the San Francisco Bay. My ambition was to build a big houseboat so I could gather all my friends to live with me rent-free. One big happy family! I guess God had other plans, however, because it wasn't the family with whom he wanted me to live. The houseboat was condemned by the city because we didn't follow the building codes. So we moved into San Francisco.

By this time, we were getting quite outrageous. Really freaky. A lot of the people who lived with us left because we were so weird. As it happened, a girl by the name of Joan left us to go to a rock concert in the state of Washington. On her way she was given a ride by some Jesus freaks who lived in Coos Bay, Oregon. Joan couldn't accept Jesus just like that. However, God was dealing with this Jewish girl. On her way through the town of Coos Bay, she was arrested for hitchhiking. The only phone number she had was of the people she had just encountered. Joan called them, and they came to bail her out.

These people lived on a ranch outside the town. Joan decided to stay over one night, but strangely enough, she stayed six months. Then Joan, having accepted Christ, wanted to share him with her good friend, my brother Fred. Fred went up to the ranch and after a time accepted the "good news."

Fred wanted to share the "good news" with me. I guess he really had a burden for me, because he came down to San Francisco to tell me about Jesus. But I didn't want to hear about Jesus. At the time I was stoned out on junk and really sick. However, I had some thoughts on it later. First of all, I was Jewish, and Jewish people don't believe such things (Joan and Fred excepted). Second, I didn't even believe in God. Third, I believed that people who believed in God were weak. They needed a crutch. I was pretty happy where I was. I wasn't being much of a problem to the world; but then again, I wasn't being much of a solution either. In any case, Jesus wasn't for me.

Fred went back to the ranch to stay. I got tired of hanging around San Francisco and figured I'd visit my brother on the ranch. I had heard a lot of things about this ranch. For one, it was out in the woods and very isolated, and I wanted to get back with nature. I started out, not knowing what I would get myself into. I'm a pretty strong-willed person, and I knew no one could convince me of something I didn't want to believe. But strangely enough, no one laid a big trip onto me. Yes, they told me about Jesus, and Bibles were lying around; but no one was twisting my arm to believe. However, I sensed something different. There were about ten young people living on the ranch. Michael and his wife, the owners, were not hippies. They had seen a need and opened their ranch to these strange-looking young people.

Out of respect for Michael, and because I wanted to understand what he was doing, I started to read the Bible. I was twenty-two years old and knew nothing about Jesus. I can remember when I was a little kid talking about him with my folks. They used to say perhaps Jesus was a rabbi or a prophet, but never, never the Son of God.

I made a mistake when I started reading the Scriptures. Some place between Matthew and Revelation, the Holy Spirit convicted me. He was dealing with me

in a strong and mighty way. I found myself doing something new—I was praying. I told God that if he were
real, I wanted to know. If there really was a God and
I didn't believe in him, I would be a fool. But I didn't
want to believe in nothing either. I had to know if he
was real. I asked him to reveal himself to me. I asked
him to raise a mountain or split some water or send
a lightning bolt and write my name in the tree.

I guess God could have done these things, but he
just doesn't work very often in that manner today. Instead, I woke up one morning and there it was!

It was like I could see for the first time in my life.
The miracle I was looking for was *us*—his creation. I
knew there was a living God. You might say, "that's
nothing," but for me it was very real. This knowledge
is what it took for God to make himself real to me.
God knows each one of us, and he knows what he has
to do in each of our lives to make us recognize him.

The first time I read the Bible was really strange.
It was like I was the first person who had ever read
this book, and I was trying to remember everything I
read so that I could relate it to other people. What made
sense to me was Jesus was a Jew, and all the claims
he made were true. I promised God that if he showed
me that he was real, I would work for him.

He kept his part of the bargain, and I'm working
on mine.

Elliott Landau

As a boy of eight, I had my initial experience with
Judaism. My mother and father wanted my two brothers
and me to be well-grounded in our religion. Realizing

their limitations to teach us, they began taking us to a synagogue. I enjoyed meeting other boys and girls and learning about God. Having nothing else to go on, I believed in God and the stories we were taught in Hebrew school. But my parents detected what they felt was a lack of interest, so they discontinued taking us.

When I was almost twelve, a regenerated interest in religion caused my parents to introduce us to a new synagogue. Contrary to my first experience in Hebrew school, this time I absorbed nothing. Our report cards were fairly good indicators of our disinterest (they usually are) and convinced my despondent parents to resign us from the class.

Shortly after this period, God revealed himself to me. I had a serious problem which I could not solve. At first, all I could do was worry. But then I began to remember some of the teaching I had learned at Hebrew school. When Israel was in trouble, they called on God for help. God had helped them through times of great conflict and trials, and I postulated that he could help me, too. I prayed, and God answered the prayer. This experience made me increasingly aware that God works in people's lives. I began to pray to God every night, asking forgiveness for when I hurt people and thanking him for what he had done.

Our family moved in 1965. The time was marked by my entrance into junior high, and the problems of puberty were joined by an additional problem of finding new friends. I stayed at home and hid behind homework. My family criticized me for using homework as a cop-out.

In high school, God brought two people into my life

who showed a special love and concern for me. One was a guy, Phil, who shared some teachers in school and moved up the street from me. The other was a girl, Marilyn, who shared some classes. During lunch, I ate with Phil and another fellow, Jeff, who was in my second Jewish Sunday School class four years earlier. It sounded like Phil tried to convert Jeff to Christianity every day. I just listened quietly, because the scope of the discussion between the two boys—each very intelligent—was uselessly beyond my theological realm.

During the school year, Phil told me quite simply that he had a personal relationship with God through Jesus Christ. I wasn't interested, but at least I had learned the definition of a Christian. Someone who accepted Christ. I refused to go to a youth group with Phil at his church when he invited me.

In the summer of 1970, Phil and I went to summer school together, and he saw me every day but never said anything further about Jesus. I began my senior year the following September, and I considered my predicament. I had tried to establish a relationship with God.

Yet the same emptiness and purposelessness remained. What was I going to do? My answer came faster than I had expected. One day I ate lunch with Phil and several new people to whom he introduced me. One of them, Don, told me about a coffee shop that his church was starting. It was to hold its grand opening the following Saturday night. He invited me to come. Not wanting to dismiss an opportunity to make new friends, I responded affirmatively and promptly arrived on Van Nuys Boulevard Saturday night to track down the correct address. Aimlessly, I stumbled into a topless bar. The usher handed back my driver's license and dollar, saying, "Sorry, son." I knew it was not the coffee shop. I meandered into the next door and found that I was in the right place. That night I listened to good musicians singing about Jesus and describing how they "invited Jesus personally into their lives as Savior and Lord." Then they related how their lives assumed a strikingly different life-style. I was given a New Testament and began to read it during the next week.

The next night I walked in the back door of the coffee shop only to notice absolute silence . . . except for the voice of one person praying. He was praying for the salvation of many souls. I wondered what it meant "to be saved."

As I pondered the matter, the entertainment commenced. During the intermission, Don introduced me to a fellow named Tom. Tom wasted no time in talking to me about Jesus. He used the term Messiah and said it was the Hebrew equivalent of Christ. Wait a minute. I had heard this term before when I inquired of my mother what she knew about such things. As the music resumed, Tom and I grabbed our chairs and proceeded outside so that we could hear our mutual speech. Tom showed me many places in the Bible where Jesus spoke. Tom also showed me how Jesus performed miracles and the many promises he made. Finally, Tom showed me striking fulfillments to prophecy made by Jewish men about a Messiah for Israel. With the same false sense of pride that prompted my parents to send me to Sunday School, I began to defend my religion. But Tom kept saying that it was part of my religion to "receive the Messiah personally."

I didn't know why I was arguing. There seemed to be more reasons for accepting Jesus as the Messiah than there were rejecting him. I said that I would like to receive Jesus, but maybe later. Tom's answer was a classic. "What if you got run over by a truck on the way home tonight and departed from this life; then it would be too late. Why postpone having the same thing that makes all these other people so happy," he asked. At this time I decided not to hesitate. "Lord Jesus, please come into my life and be my personal Savior and Lord and show me the forgiveness and victory in life that you promised and the eternal life that you spoke of. Amen."

Now I claim the truth of 2 Corinthians 5:17: "Therefore if any man be in Christ, he is a new creature: old things are passed away; behold, all things are become new." In Jesus Christ I have found the ultimate experience with God, to share in his satisfying riches of love through the cross that Jesus Christ endured for our sakes. God has helped me to overcome the loneliness that once plagued my life. The emptiness is so full of God's love that I desire to share it with all of you who read this story. But just as one must take a gift to possess it, so you must accept this gift of everlasting life from the real Giver, our God and Creator. I guarantee that it will be yours, and that you will experience the same pardon, power, and purpose in life as I have, as freely and abundantly as Jesus Christ lived and died to give it. Really, God's thing is love. Jesus proves it.

Steffi Geiser

I am a nice Jewish girl from the Bronx. I was brought up in a neighborhood that was 99 percent Jewish, and I don't think I ever met the other 1 percent. I grew up thinking that we were a majority group. During my elementary school years, I attended Yiddish school every day after my regular classes for five years. There I learned to read and write Yiddish and to appreciate the culture and history of my people.

I went to a specialized high school called the Bronx High School of Science, which was also a highly Jewish institution. I was competitive by nature and success-oriented and did well in school. I switched from the study of science to the arts during my senior year.

I went directly to college with my 96-point average. The college I chose was a local one; and because it had a rather poor art department, when the English Department took an interest in me, I thought for sure it would be just a matter of time till I would write the great American (great Bronx?) novel. I left college to try out the real world and became a secretary. I couldn't type (the peck-peck method did not impress anyone in the business world), and I couldn't take shorthand. But I was nineteen and the only young person in the old-man world of corporate business, and they kept me on for six months. Then I was "discovered." While sending around little "arty" messages from office to office, someone in the display end of the organization arranged an interview with the president of a display company downtown in New York. I went to the interview a little frightened, very wet behind the ears, with a thrown-together portfolio and a hope-against-hope wonderment about what it would be like to do something I enjoyed for a living. Amazed, I found myself instantly hired.

About the time I began to work in art, I also began to get into drugs, mostly marijuana and some LSD. The experiences I felt at the time enhanced my artistic attitude. But I also found my drive, my achievement- and accomplishment-oriented nature was slipping into dullness. I began to lack ambition. The lethargy was almost welcome. I began to wonder about God.

Oddly enough, it was not in a Jewish context that my questioning began. It was not the "Jewish God" that I was looking for. My Jewishness had long since lapsed into the stage of simply taking off work on the Jewish holidays and going to the movies in celebration of Yom Kippur. I began reading Edgar Cayce, the clairvoyant, who claimed to know all kinds of things about God, Jesus, reincarnation, dreams, dieting, and healing processes. I also explored the realms of Zen and the writings of both modern-day psychologists and ancient thinkers. I could go along with much of what some of them said, but nothing that I read impressed me enough to "change my life."

Although designing was about the epitome of what I could ever desire for a job, the point of the whole idea became meaningless to me. I found myself being more and more stoned, less and less interested in fashion and status.

WHY spend money to advertise women's clothing and children's toys and household appliances in colors to match your very own kitchen? What was the point? I decided to go back to being a kid, and so I enrolled in the University of Buffalo, bent upon leaving New

York City, leaving the big, bad business world, and leaving my parents' house.

When Christmas vacation came, a friend and I decided to go to the West Coast. We arrived on January 1, 1971. I remember thinking: Ah, a new year, I wonder. . . . I was immediately disappointed in San Francisco and Berkeley. Where was the sunshine? How come people weren't surfing in the Pacific Ocean? Why didn't anyone tell me that it *rains* in San Francisco in January! I was ready to go back to Buffalo, I was so disappointed. About the fourth day I was in Berkeley, my friend and I were accosted by two overanxious old friends of hers who had recently come to know Jesus, the Son of God. That was very nice, I assured them; but since I was Jewish, it hardly interested me. Now, that pronouncement surprised nobody more than it did me. It had been years since expressing my Jewishness to anyone. But I figured it was the most efficient way I could think of to turn off a couple of overly emphatic Jesus freaks. "Hallelujah!" they said. "That's wonderful!"

"That's what?" I asked. "That's not *anything*. That's just what I am." I certainly was not excited about my Jewishness and it slightly unnerved me that they should be. They invited me to a Bible study which they said was being taught by this Jewish guy, and it was about Jesus. Well, I thought: "Even if there are no surfers in San Francisco, here, at least is something to write home about." I figured I had now heard everything. So I went.

After the study, the teacher came up to me and showed me a few passages in, to my surprise, the Old Testament. What he should be doing with an Old Testament I didn't

understand. I thought that Jesus was only in the New
Testament. The passages he showed me seemed to speak
of suffering and sin, but I had to tell him: "Look, I
know that you're gonna tell me that the punch line to
this is *Jesus,* but if I told you I believed that, I'd be
lying, 'cause I don't."

The teacher asked me what I thought God wanted
me to do. I said that I thought he wanted me to read
the Bible. Now this was my second surprising declaration
of the day, because I didn't exactly believe in God!
But I figured I owed it to myself to take a good look
at the Bible.

I was troubled with what I read the next few days.
It wasn't any one passage that impressed me. It was
a person. I couldn't understand Jesus. He wasn't like
me. He wasn't like anyone I'd met or read about. I
didn't want to believe this gospel that I had begun to
take seriously. But I couldn't ignore the impact the words
were making upon me. Someone in the house suggested
that I might ask God to make himself real through his
Word. I sat in a room and shocked myself a third time
by talking to God. I wasn't very polite.

"OK, God . . . If you're real, I want to know it. If
this book I'm reading isn't just another interesting story,
but is the truth, then I'll believe it. But I'm not going
to believe in nothing. You've gotta show me."

"You've gotta. . . ." That's a nice way to talk to God,
right? But the strange thing is that he did make himself
quite real to me. After a couple of days of feeling trapped
and freed simultaneously, I couldn't deny that God was
real and that the Bible was true. The things I read in
the Old Testament spoke of the same Messiah that I

read about in the New. I knew that indeed the "punch line" was Jesus.

On January 10, I committed my life to Jesus, knowing that there would be no one who would be happy for me among my friends and family. I remained in California and lived at the house for the next four months, cooking meals for the Jewish and Gentile believers who were learning much about Jewishness and the God of the Bible. I began to appreciate my Jewish education and my Jewish heritage in a new way. It had to do with *today* for the first time in my life. The people of yesterday lived for me as I began my new life. The Messiah of Israel had indeed come.

Bill Katin

When I was young, I remember asking my mother if Jesus was the Messiah. She said no, and at that time, the answer satisfied me.

During high school, I felt that I was open-minded, so I would talk to my friends about Jesus and other religious topics. However, the truth was that I loved to argue. One day after math class, a girl named Sharon came up to me and started talking to me.

After getting to know her better, I asked her out. She told me that she didn't want to go out with any guy who wasn't a Christian. Her response surprised me. I thought she had "flipped her lid." I went home thinking that I was a good, moral, Jewish boy, and perhaps that made me a Christian. I looked the word up in the dictionary, and it said, "one who was a follower of Jesus." I knew that wasn't me, because I hated Jesus. I determined right away that I couldn't become a Christian just to please her. But I had debated with my other friends, so I felt I might as well find out what she believed.

We began meeting every day for lunch. Then I discovered my physics teacher was also a Christian. I was stunned. I could not believe that anyone that intelligent could possibly be a Christian.

During this one-year period, I was going to the hospital twice a month for an acute kidney infection. Once, and only once, I prayed to the God of Abraham, Isaac, and Jacob, saying that if Jesus of Nazareth was the promised Messiah, to make me well this one time, and I would believe. It was the only time I ever prayed that prayer, and it was the only time I was better. However, I reneged on my promise. I refused to believe.

As time passed, tears would come into my eyes while talking to Sharon, knowing that what she was saying was true; but I could not admit it. Then one evening, I remember calling her and telling her that I believed that Jesus was the Messiah, and that I wanted to invite him into my life.

Since then my life has really changed. Now I have a peace and joy about life that I never had before accepting the Messiah.

David Schoenberg

I was brought up in a Reform home. The religious training I received was not because I wanted it, but because my grandfather had insisted on it. I attended eight years of Saturday school, three years of Hebrew school, and was Bar Mitzvahed.

After my Bar Mitzvah, I lived a life for no one but

myself, Dave Schoenberg. I had never heard about Christ until my senior year in high school when I attended a concert at a Christian coffeehouse.

I met a lot of other students at the coffeehouse. They seemed different. They were friendlier, not just among themselves, but also with me. I asked what it was all about, and they told me it was the love of Jesus Christ. My puzzled response was, "What's a Jesus Christ?"

They proceeded to explain, but I couldn't accept it. It went totally against everything I had learned at temple, but something kept compelling me to go back. Tormenting me. I even went to a few Bible studies to ask questions and find out more. The following January I received a New Testament and started reading it until the end of March, when I received a whole Bible for my birthday. Then I discontinued reading the New Testament and started reading the Old Testament.

Why was I doing all this reading? Because I was trying to find out for myself who this Jesus was they were talking about.

I was searching for the hub of a wheel. The spokes were there. They were all the bits and pieces I had heard and read during the past six months. The week before I was to graduate from high school, I was driving home and thinking about all the things I had heard. It seemed strange, God's love and forgiveness, God's "dumb" idea of sending someone to die for everyone else. But it didn't seem so "dumb" anymore. Jesus fit every qualification that God had set up for the sacrificial system of the Old Testament. It finally dawned on me that Jesus was the hub of my broken wheel. All the spokes came together in Jesus.

Before I got home that night, I had accepted Christ into my life, to lead it, to rule it, and to mold it to what He wanted it to be. All this was said in the simple words, "God, I'll give it a try."

Conclusion

Jews who have faced Jesus and come to know him in a real and personal way all testify to the fact that Jesus did bring them justification, spiritual healing, and reconciliation with God. This is what the Old Testament said the death and resurrection of Messiah would accomplish, and this is what the New Testament says Jesus did accomplish. Jewish lives that have been changed by Jesus all testify that not only did Jesus enhance their Jewishness, but that Jesus is the Jew's Jew.

ABOUT THE AUTHOR

Dr. Arnold G. Fruchtenbaum was born in Russia after his parents were released from a Communist prison. With the help of the Israeli underground, the Fruchtenbaum family escaped from behind the Iron Curtain. Fruchtenbaum received Orthodox Jewish training while living in Germany from 1947 to 1951, when he and his family finally immigrated to New York.

Dr. Fruchtenbaum is the founder and director of Ariel Ministries, headquartered in Tustin, California. He is a graduate of Cedarville College in Ohio and earned his Th.M. at Dallas Theological Seminary in Texas and his Ph.D. at New York University. His graduate work includes studies at the Jewish Theological Seminary in New York City and the Hebrew University in Jerusalem. He has also been nominated as one of the nation's "Outstanding Young Men."

He lived in Israel for three years, two of them with his wife, Mary Ann. During his time there, the historic Six-Day War broke out between Israel and the Arab nations. His first-hand observation of this critical period in Israel's history, as well as his intensive study of the role of the nation of Israel in God's plan of world redemption, has made him a popular speaker and teacher at Bible conferences throughout the United States and the world. He has authored a number of books and pamphlets of keen interest to both Jews and Gentiles.